ZEN BUDDHISM

Beliefs and Practices

MERV FOWLER

sussex
ACADEMIC
PRESS

BRIGHTON • *PORTLAND*

2 4 6 8 10 9 7 5 3 1

First published 2005 in Great Britain by
SUSSEX ACADEMIC PRESS
Box 2950
Brighton BN2 5SP

and in the United States of America by
SUSSEX ACADEMIC PRESS
920 NE 58th Ave Suite 300
Portland, Oregon 97213–3786

British Library Cataloguing in Publication Data
A CIP catalogue record for this book is available from the British Library.

Library of Congress Cataloging-in-Publication Data
Fowler, Merv.
    Zen Buddhism : beliefs and practices / Merv
Fowler.
    p. cm.
Includes bibliographical references and index.
    ISBN 1-902210-42-5 (pbk. : alk. paper)
    1. Zen Buddhism. I. Title.
BQ9265.4.F68 2005
294.3'927—dc22

2005005584

Typeset by G&G Editorial, Brighton & Eastbourne
Printed by TJ International, Padstow, Cornwall
This book is printed on acid-free paper.

Contents

Preface and Acknowledgements		vii
Abbreviations		ix
	Introduction	1
	***Part I* Zen Beliefs**	
1	The Ox-herding Pictures	13
2	Zen Roots	25
	The legacy of India	27
	The life of the Buddha	31
	The account of the Buddha's life in the Buddhacarita *and other sources*	32
3	Doctrines Germane to Zen	44
	The dharma *of the Buddha*	45
	The First Noble Truth	46
	The five aggregates	49
	The Second Noble Truth	51
	Dependent Origination	53
	The Third Noble Truth	55
	The Fourth Noble Truth	56
	The Pancha Sila	61
	Sila, Samadhi, Panna	63
4	Zen and the Mahayana Sutras	68
	Sunyata	72
	Zen and Yoga	73

5   Buddhism Reaches China   76
    Bodhidharma   79
    Hui-k'o   82
    Hui-neng   84
    The Zen Movement after Hui-neng   86
    The Five Houses   92
        Kuei-yang   93
        Lin-chi   93
        Ts'ao-tung   94
        Yun-men   94
        Fa-yen   94
    The Sung Period   95

6   The Transition from China to Japan   97
    The cultural influence of Rinzai Zen   97
    Myoan Eisai   99
    Enni Ben'en   100
    Dogen Kigen   101
    Zen after Dogen   102

Part II   Zen Practice

7   Meditation   109
    The theory   110
    The practice   111
    Zazen   113
    Kensho   114
    Soto Zen   116
    Monks and monasteries   117

8   Koan Practice   125
9   The Master–Pupil Relationship   134
    Dokusan   140
    Kyosaku   140

10 Holding the Mind   143

Notes   149
Glossary   158
Further Reading   165
Index   168

Preface and Acknowledgements

This work is the culmination of years of teaching, study and conversations with many Buddhist friends, scholars, and students. Their contribution is immeasurable, though any misunderstandings and errors remain my own. I am grateful to the Reverend Leandra at Throssel Hole Buddhist Abbey for her immediate responses to my questions, and to Brian Gay, a lay minister of the Order of Buddhist Contemplatives, and former neighbour. My understanding of Buddhism in general and Soto Zen in particular has been greatly enhanced by the many forest conversations we held while walking our (now sadly departed) dogs over the course of twenty years living next door to one another. As always, Jim Pym of the Pure Land Buddhist Fellowship has been swift to help and slow to criticize, answering my queries and drawing my attention to books of which I would otherwise have remained in ignorance.

I am particularly grateful to Anthony Grahame, Editorial Director at Sussex Academic Press, whose patience and understanding bear full testimony to the publisher's claim to be "author friendly". Tony has waited a long time for this book, but never once did he attempt to pressurize me to submit until I was ready.

The Library and Learning Resources staff on the Caerleon campus at the University of Wales, Newport have given every assistance in the production of this book. The library collection of works on Buddhism in stock is considerable, and I am deeply indebted, as always, to Lesley May (Deputy Head of LLR) and, more recently, Wyn Thomas, for effectuating this. Nigel Twomey has been invaluable in securing inter-library loan facilities promptly and efficiently. I am also extremely grateful to Sarah Norman at the Institute of Oriental Philosophy

European Centre for locating many texts on Zen and allowing me free access to the extensive library facilities at Taplow Court, Berkshire.

The Ox-herding pictures are reproduced courtesy of Kazuaki Tanahashi.

The enso or Zen circle, used as the chapter opening page design, has been described by Sherry Chayat, art critic for *The Syracuse Herald American*, as "multi-directional, flowing, often asymmetrical, unpredictable. It is not a representation, but an unmediated experience of the present moment, which has no beginning, no end, no limitation, and no unchanging form . . . [it] represents the interconnectedness of all life, and closes the illusory gap between artistic endeavor and spiritual truth, between metaphysical investigation and community engagement."

In my final year of teaching at the University of Wales, Newport, I had the extreme good fortune to teach the best group of MA students and the best group of final year undergraduate students that I have known in twelve years at the University. The contribution these students made to my own well-being and my understanding of life is immeasurable. They are too numerous to name individually though I shall always remember Ted in the MA group, a man who was far more concerned with what he could put into life than what he could get out of it; perhaps we can all learn from people such as Ted.

Of the final year undergraduate students, Stuart, Shahid, David and Martin stood out from the men, whilst three young ladies were very special students to me. There is a saying, "If blessed, you will meet someone who touches your life immeasurably." If this is so, then I have been thrice blessed. Readers of this book will soon become familiar with the Triple Treasure, the cornerstone of Buddhist practice, but I have been blessed with my own triple treasure, and it is to Kerry, Beth and Becky that I dedicate this book in deep gratitude and affection.

MERV FOWLER. NEWPORT, SEPTEMBER 2004

Abbreviations

Diacritical marks for transliterated text have not been used in this student edition. The following abbreviations may not be familiar to every reader:

BCE   before common (or Christian) era
CE   common (or Christian) era
Skt   Sanskrit
Jap.   Japanese
Chin.   Chinese
Dhp   the *Dhammapada*, one of the books of the *Khaddaka Nikaya*, the fifth major division of the *Sutta Pitaka* in the Pali canon.

The Pali word *nikaya* means "collection" and the following letters refer to the appropriate *nikaya* or collection from the Pali Canon:

D   *Digha Nikaya*
M   *Majjhima Nikaya*
A   *Anguttara Nikaya*
S   *Samyutta Nikaya*

Introduction

The dualism of yin and yang, which rules the cosmos under the conciliating influence of the Tao, exists in man as it does in the rest of creation. Our awareness of this dualism is expressed in the belief that we are made of two autonomous elements, which we refer to variously as body and soul, matter and spirit, instinct and reason, etc. A whole range of common expressions reflect this belief in our two-part composition: '*I* am master of *myself*', '*I* cannot stop *myself*', '*I* am pleased with *myself*', '*I* am fed up with *myself*', etc.[1]

For those of us who wend our way through each day, constantly searching for something to worry about,[2] there is always the "reassurance" that all is not well. There is something *lacking* within us that prevents us from feeling complete – making us dissatisfied with life in general and ourselves in particular. It is this supposed deficit, that we all recognize, to which Zen Buddhism directs its attention. Some years ago, I invited a recovering alcoholic to the University to address a group of students. He began by asking whether it is we who control our minds or whether our minds control us. A startled student looked up and exclaimed, "But they are one and the same thing!"

To the eastern way of thinking, she was right, but the western mind thinks differently. We have no problem accepting that we are made up of various parts – muscles, bones, joints, limbs, organs *etc.*, but that not one of these parts, or indeed all of them together, could ever be said to constitute *us*. However, we don't think like this when we consider the mind. Were we to arrange to meet a colleague at the railway station who is a stranger to us and, on the walk to the car, she happened to observe that we did not appear to be walking normally, this would surely cause no offence. We would simply assure her that she was mistaken, or explain the reason for our limp. Were the same colleague to remark that we did not appear to be *thinking* properly, however, this is a different matter altogether, obviously intended as a personal insult for, *we are what we think*. It is not without significance that there is no word in the English language for both body and mind.

> This typical Western misunderstanding blocks access to the authentic character of Eastern meditation, which is always concerned with the entire (physical and mental) person and knows nothing of the dualism of body and soul that stems from Greek philosophy. In the Asian outlook there is no separate body; the human being is at once body and soul, with the bodily and the mental united as a whole.[3]

At another point in the aforementioned lecture, the speaker was asked, "Were you to take just one sip of a very weak table wine, would you then be in trouble?" I can remember his exact words to this day. "Oh, no," he replied . . . "I would be in trouble a long time before that!" It is sobering indeed to recognize that we live our lives continually oppressed, not by an objective world, but by our deluded minds.

The Deluded Mind

> You may take the most gallant sailor, the most intrepid airman, or the most audacious soldier, put them at a table together – what do you get? *The sum of their fears.*
>
> WINSTON CHURCHILL ON THE CHIEFS OF STAFFS SYSTEM,
16 NOVEMBER 1943

It is our perceptions of real and imagined threats that generate our anxieties, not an objective appraisal of the situation. A ringing doorbell will be interpreted in different ways in different mindsets; to a mother anxiously awaiting a phone call from her son, away on his first skiing holiday since an earlier (near fatal) accident, the peal will bring fear and dread, while her daughter who is anticipating her first date will be filled with excitement. A request to visit the line-manager's office at the end of the day could well mean good news, but until we enter that room, our minds are riven with anxiety. This fear may manifest itself in multifarious forms, including defensive or indifferent behaviour before a supervisor who simply wished to seek our advice on a matter that had nothing whatever to do with our employment. The letter from the Inland Revenue, that could well contain a cheque, remains unopened for days, because we have pre-empted its content, anticipating that it can only bring bad news; unanswered phone calls and unopened e-mails are treated likewise for similar reasons.

It has been well said that a wife is someone who can look in a drawer and find a pair of socks that aren't there, but husbands do not hold the rights to myopia. Areas of our mind have the capacity to be closed down (much like Hal in *2001 Space Odyssey*) when confronted with what the mind considers to be "unacceptable" information. Forty years after the assassination of President Kennedy, not one name has been put forward as an accomplice to Lee Harvey Oswald. Despite this, the American public at large still prefers to accept the so-called "Conspiracy Theory" over and against the detailed and prolonged findings of the Warren Report. Much more recent inquiries that have dismissed criticisms of the American and British Governments have suffered a similar fate.

The greater our anxiety, the more blinkered we become; consequently, we are left with the vision to see only one side of the proverbial coin. We need not look beyond the fond perceptions that we have created of police speed cameras, that we have all come to know and love, to see that this is so. The sighting, and subsequent reporting, of a white van (that didn't happen to be the same one) at several of the scenes of crime visited by the Washington sniper was taken to establish beyond cavil the identity of the murderer's vehicle. Although there are innumerable vans being driven through the streets of Washington (white being their most common colour), this did not register with us. At the same time, the fact that a red car (that undoubtedly *was* the same one) was present at each and every shooting went unnoticed. This lack of total vision has ramifications. We invariably criticise the weaknesses that we (partially) see in others, at the same time excusing our own shortcomings as "good intentions". How often have we said, "It's all your fault", "Now look what you've made me do", "He spoilt my evening" or "She's ruining my life"? But we need no help from others. We are eminently capable of ruining our own lives, dutifully informed by our own tunnel vision. Perhaps we are too quick to apportion blame to others. I think it was Steven Wright who once said,

> Never criticize a man until you have walked a mile in his shoes. Then, if he gets angry, he'll be a mile away and barefooted.

How often have we behaved badly, not because we are being threatened, but because we have demonized an issue where there was no confrontation in mind . . . apart from *our* minds? Research by Daniel Goleman has identified the human condition as having, in a sense, *two* minds, the rational mind and the emotional mind, one that thinks and one that feels.[4] Accordingly, we develop two different kinds of intelligence, rational and emotional. Ironically, it is not the rational mind, with its capacity for reason, deliberation and reflection that is the more powerful facet of the thinking process, but the impulsive, often illogical emotional mind, that can, and often does, overcome rational thought. We can recognize Goleman's thesis[5] in our daily behaviour. We are at our most vulnerable when we anticipate confrontation. Our neighbour is sure to react badly when we make a perfectly reasonable complaint, so we predict the response and rehearse the anticipated dialogue *ad nauseam*. When the response *is* reasonable, we fail to recognize it and continue to develop our argument. We behave similarly when we wish to return unwanted goods to the store.

Buddhism in general and Zen Buddhism in particular pay great attention to the deluded mind. Interestingly, one contemporary Zen master attests the first of four modest aims for beginners on retreat as being able *to realize that one is not in control of one's own mind.*[6] Equally interestingly, when the much-maligned "man-in-the-street" is asked to name but one school of Buddhism, he invariably answers "Zen", while other schools remain quite unknown to him. Most westerners feel they have at least some familiarity with the way of Zen, a phrase that chimes to western ears. Popular images of Zen gardens, Zen masters, martial arts, monks, meditation, even Japanese Tea ceremonies, spring readily to mind; yet Zen is arguably the least understood of all the Mahayana schools.

The problem of understanding Zen correctly has not been helped by the popular misconception that Zen is "pure experience", beyond religion, beyond philosophy, beyond doctrine, no more Buddhist than any other religion. But if this is untrue, then what *is* the way of Zen? In a sense, this raises more questions than answers, because it is our obsession with bringing an end to suffering by addressing a problem that doesn't exist that is the root cause of the very suffering that we are trying to alleviate. Man's inherent desire to identify and follow *the correct path* stems from an overwhelming conviction that all is not well within his being; having reached this conclusion, obviously the first step is to recognize what is wrong and then *do* something about it. In so doing, man is transformed into some egotistical actor, playing out a part for which no words have been written, yet one in which he is the author of his own destiny. Far from alleviating suffering, however, this conviction has quite the opposite effect, as noted by Reverend Master Daishin Morgan, incumbent abbot at Throssel Hole Soto Zen Priory in Northumberland:

> What is a feature of probably everyone who comes to Buddhism . . . is the fact that they experience suffering on some level or another, and as far as Buddhism is concerned, the cause of that suffering is ignorance, in that because we don't understand what it is that we do, we create consequences that produce suffering for ourselves and for others.[7]

We all recognize that there are times when we cannot explain why we behave in a certain way. There is a strange irony about an intelligent human being paying a fortune to fly to the other side of the world, in a machine costing millions of pounds, willingly undergoing a series of rigorous security checks, not to mention body searches, in order to splash about in a rock-pool looking for seashells.[8] But perhaps this is an example of movement towards the state of "childlikeness" referred to at the start of the chapter on the Ox-herding pictures, a state of mind wholly conducive to the realization of enlightenment. At other times, we cannot explain why we *react* in a certain way; what is it precisely that is responsible for our mood swings? Much of the problem is caused by the baggage that we all carry; sometimes this baggage is hard to bear. We pick up cues as we go through each day, and as these cues remind us (often, subconsciously) of the past, we respond accordingly. I recall Francis Rossi, of *Status Quo* fame, saying how much he loved his father who, in turn, idolized his, once small, son. Mr Rossi was an ice-cream vendor who, on hot days would be on the road very early in order to support his family. On warm summer evenings he would not return home until late, far too late for little Francis to be awake. Conversely, wet miserable days would herald the prospect of spending all day long with his small son, a situation that brought great joy to them both. The point is that even today, decades later, Francis still feels cheerful when he is awakened to the sound of rain lashing the windows or a biting wind rattling the panes, and depressed when the sun bursts into his room in the early morning.

Since we know ourselves better than anyone else (so the argument goes), clearly we are the ones best suited to identify the problem and rectify it. The teaching of Zen is that suffering is not caused by the fact that each individual has something inherently wrong within, but because we are quite unaware that there is *nothing* wrong that needs to be put right. In this light, Zen training is not about striving above all else to seek enlightenment, but shaving away ego-centred thoughts until one recognizes that one lacks *nothing*. In the words of the French psychologist, Hubert Benoit:

> everything seems to be going wrong in me because the fundamental idea that everything is perfectly, eternally and totally positive is dormant in the centre of my being, instead of being awake, alive and active.[9]

On his awakening, the Buddha, Sakyamuni, made the self-same point: "How wonderful, how miraculous – all beings are fully endowed with the Tathagata's (Buddha's) wisdom and power, but sadly, because of their attachments, human beings are not aware of this." Appropriately, after his Enlightenment, the Buddha was asked, "Are you a God?" Sakyamuni said he was not. "Are you a saint?" Again the answer was in the negative. "Then what are you?" persisted his questioner. And he answered, "I am awake." To "awaken" in Zen is to free oneself from the habitual clutter of a fantasizing mind, and live "in our bodies, in the moment". We spend so much time living outside our bodies. Early morning visitors to gymnasia throughout the world will readily identify with this, as their cheerful "Good mornings" (in languages various) fall on deaf ears in the changing rooms, the clientele having time and space only to consider the next target as they prepare to leave the gym for work.

As surely as mankind deludes itself that all is not well, so does it suffer from the illusion that, in order to achieve liberation, it needs to free itself from the chains that keep it in shackles. Ironically, as long as man feels duty-bound to achieve his own salvation, he will remain precisely that, *bound* and as free from liberation as ever. What has to be discarded is the delusion that there is the *need* to free oneself and the attendant duty of salvation. Mankind will be free as soon as it awakens to the fact that it is free already – there are no shackles.

At this point, the reader could be forgiven for wondering, if there is no need to free oneself, no real need to *do anything*, then how can there be a need for Zen Buddhism; surely, in the enlightenment of twenty-first century "civilization", we are eminently capable of addressing any problems that may arise? Perhaps the reader would also like to ponder over the words of Juliette Boutonnier, who claims that we do not know how to cope with life: "our civilization, which often fails to teach us how to live, is no better at teaching us how to die. It provides morphine to ease suffering in the final stages of life, and that is virtually all."[10] Every sentient being, of necessity, has both a birthday and a deathday; we rejoice in the former and ignore the latter, which is unattested in the English language.

D. T. Suzuki was probably the greatest single influence in bringing Zen Buddhism to the West. He was once said to have given the West nine-tenths of all it knows on the subject.[11] This is what he had to say about Zen teaching:

> If I am asked, then, what Zen teaches, I would answer Zen teaches nothing. Whatever teachings there are in Zen, they come out of one's own mind. We teach ourselves; Zen merely points the way.[12]

We begin our journey by treading the calf path, or rather the ox path, with the beast's wandering tracks depicting our wayward minds as we meander our way along life's path. *Samsara* means "aimless wandering", an apt description of the continuing cycle of death and rebirth that we all endure. Perhaps it is also a good description of how we approach life. Maybe we can learn something from the parable of the Ox-herding pictures, ten pictorial representations of our gradual development from aimless wandering towards Buddhahood.

Chapter 2, "Zen Roots", recognizes that Zen Buddhism was not conceived in a vacuum. The popular notion that Zen is not a child of Buddhism but an orphan, rejoicing in the name of "Pure Experience", is examined critically. Accordingly, Zen Buddhism is placed in its historical context and the evidence examined responsibly. The legacy of India is accredited and the life of the Buddha revisited, as we consider the precise nature and purpose of the founder of Buddhism.

In Chapter 3, entitled "Doctrines Germane to Zen", we look at the teachings of the Buddha, Sakyamuni, analysing what he actually said. We look at the Four Noble Truths and The Noble Eightfold Path, among others, and see whether his teaching has anything to offer us today, or whether it is really for those people who lived all those years ago, or at least live all those miles away.

Chapter 4, "Zen and the Mahayana Sutras", looks at the Scriptures themselves. Like many great religious leaders, the Buddha wrote nothing. Everything the Buddha taught was delivered orally, and it was four centuries before a supposedly complete record of his teachings was produced. The most important Mahayana literature for Zen Buddhism is the *Prajnaparamita* literature, the "Perfection of Wisdom". The concept of emptiness, *sunyata*, which is fundamental to Zen Buddhism, is also examined, as is the relationship between Zen and yoga.

In Chapter 5, "Buddhism reaches China", we look at the advent of Buddhism in mainland China. Far from being a seamless transmission, the problems for which Buddhism offered solutions were not Chinese problems. The Indian mind was preoccupied with suffering, its cause and its cure, a concern that had never arisen in Chinese thought, so what did Buddhism have to offer a people who were not like-minded?

Chapter 6 attests the transition of Zen Buddhism from China to Japan, examining the claim that "The Zen masters contributed nothing substantial to the teachings and methods of Zen". The most influential figure in Japan's religious thought was Great Master Dogen Kigen. Ironically, Dogen had no wish to introduce a new form of Buddhism to Japan, yet it was he who brought Soto Zen to Japan from China.

Part II of this book is concerned with Zen practice in daily life. It opens by looking at "Meditation", both in theory and practice. Various terms are explained and examined including *satori, kensho* and *zazen*. Problems that face the meditator are considered, as is the need to meditate and the contribution that meditation has to offer. What on earth does the ego have to do with all of this?

Chapter 8 is devoted entirely to *koan* practice. We look at the purpose and function of the *koan* device, as well as questioning some popular interpretations. Is the koan really a riddle wrapped in a mystery inside an enigma?

In Chapter 9 we look at the master–pupil relationship in Zen Buddhism. Is this fundamental to the school or not? If one wishes to become a student of Zen Buddhism, is having a personal tutor, a Zen master, a prerequisite?

Finally, in a chapter entitled "Holding the Mind" we analyse the problems facing the would-be newcomer to Zen training.

It is hoped that the American reader will find much of interest in these pages. The thoughts of *Roshi* Philip Kapleau, the much loved and recently departed founder of the Rochester Zen Center in upstate New York, permeate this book, while space is given also to those who credit his breadth of thinking. There are numerous references to Shasta Abbey, the Soto Zen abbey on Mount Shasta, California, and to its founder, Reverend Master Jiyu-Kennett. Professor John Koller's contribution to understanding the Oriental mind is immense, and his work as Professor of Asian and Comparative Philosophy at the Rensselaer Polytechnic Institute in Troy, New York, is credited in the section "Further Reading". I learned recently from a private communication with Professor Koller that he has been practising for more than forty years.

It has been well said that eastern thought lies beyond the compass of the western mind. This is true of how we view ourselves. The westerner regards his body as a car, to be driven to extremes in order (supposedly) to gain maximum benefit from it. When this body is in need of repair, he takes it to the coachbuilders (which he calls a surgery) and confronts the doctor, whom he treats as a mechanic. If an accurate diagnosis, with accompanying prescription and subsequent cure, is not forthcoming immediately, the physician is considered to be incompetent. If the complaint is later identified as chronic, then clearly the doctor is unsuited to his profession and deserves to be "struck off"; either way, there is the tacit inference that the doctor is in some way responsible for the ailment. The eastern mind, on the other hand, regards the *body and mind* as a fragile garden, to be tended and cared for, watered and rested, loved and cherished. The westerner may well admire a Zen garden, but may be curious about its function. If it is not a children's playground or an area for walking the dog, then what is it? He could be forgiven for concluding that its purpose is to stimulate the mind, but if this is his interpretation then he is simply wrong. The Zen Buddhist will be all too aware that the purpose of the garden is not to stimulate the mind but to still it. If the westerner feels that his eyes are tired he will close and rest them, but what if the same is true of his mind? What the easterner does . . . is contained in the pages of this modest book.

Part I
Zen Beliefs

Despite all the efforts of Zen experts . . . the insight afforded us Europeans into the essence of Zen has remained exceedingly scanty. As though it resisted deeper penetration, after a few steps one's groping intuition comes up against insurmountable barriers. Wrapped in impenetrable darkness, Zen must seem the strangest riddle which the spiritual life of the East has ever devised; insoluble yet irresistibly attractive.[1]

1 The Ox-herding Pictures

Man is a thinking reed but his great works are done when he is not calculating and thinking. "Childlikeness" has to be restored after long years of training in the art of self-forgetfulness. When this is attained, man thinks yet he does not think. He thinks like the showers coming down from the sky; he thinks like the waves rolling in the ocean; he thinks like the green foliage shooting forth in the relaxing spring breeze. Indeed, he is the showers, the ocean, the stars, the foliage. When a man reaches this stage of "spiritual" development, he is a Zen artist of life. He does not need, like the painter, a canvas, brushes, and paints; nor does he require, like the archer, the bow and arrow and target, and other paraphernalia.[2]

To return to the question of what the deluded mind has to do with Buddhism, the answer is "Everything!" for *Buddhism is a mind-culture.* In this light, it is fitting that we begin to tread the path of Zen with the parable of the Ox-herding pictures, ten pictorial representations of the developing relationship between our Buddha-nature (the Ox) and ourselves (the Ox-herd). Since the time of the Sung dynasty in China, the path taken by the Zen practitioner has been depicted in pictorial terms, along with associated interpretations, poems and commentaries. There are four well-known versions, some of which portray a darkened ox in the first picture, (representing an ignorant, deluded mind) that lightens along its journey, as we gradually awaken to our own true (Buddha) nature. It is fitting that an animal so common in ancient China should be used in a parable that could be meaningful to the common man.

1 The Search for the Ox

Distant mountains, deep waters, dense forests
conceal the tracks of the ox.
The way is unclear and the mind exhausted.
Listen instead to the chirping of insects.

We recognize that within us lies the propensity to look for something to worry about. Often, we have no idea of the cause of this unease, but since we recognize it, clearly, it must be real. Accordingly, we need to act, but not knowing what it is that we have to do, we act badly and bring suffering upon ourselves. Even when our circumstances are favourable, and we are blessed with good health, loving relationships, and rewarding employment, none of these can possibly last forever, so this is the seedbed for further anxiety.

2 Finding traces

Deep within the forest echoes the faint murmur of running water.
Traces are found, but is this the right path?
The mountains are endless and the sky distant.
How can the ox keep the tip of its nose from sight?

This is the first glimpse of a way forward that could alleviate our unease. The tracks are erratic, but so is our mind. We now hear about Zen, and even read a little. The stress of everyday life seems far removed from Zen when we learn about it from a practitioner, but we stop there. We simply get a warm feeling of something new, but how old are the footprints? Is this really for us? How can we be sure?

3　The Sighting

Among willow branches, a nightingale sings cheerfully.
The willows are green, the sun warm, the breeze gentle.
Alone in the thicket, the ox is glimpsed,
with stately horns and majestic head.

With the first glimpse of the Ox, comes the realization that now is the time for real commitment; simply hearing about Zen is not good enough. We may continue to read about Zen, but now there must be more, so we experiment. We take on board the Buddhist Precepts and even visit a Zen Centre, for here we can learn about meditation. We now recognize that we need help; without it we are little more than victims of our thoughts, prisoners of our culture. Certainly, we can all choose which subject we wish to consider, but we have no control whatever over what thoughts come to mind, and we have to take them as they come; surely this is what Zen training is all about?

4 Capture

At last the ox is caught, though your energy is sapped.
But its will is strong, its power uncontrollable.
You are dragged in its wake
through mountain pass and misty glade.

The Ox is captured and so is our interest, but in many ways capture is the easy part. Both the Ox and our minds are wayward creatures that need to be harnessed, for they each want to go their own way. The Ox will constantly pull this way and that with a force equal to that which diverts our concentration away from meditation. The directions appear easy at first, the application anything but. The physical discomfort of sitting in an unaccustomed position for a period of time is disconcerting enough, but it is not only our bodies that are unused to stillness. Our mind, too, reacts to quietness, preferring instead to ferret around in search of an idea, and when it has found one, developing thought upon thought, and pulling each in its wake like the proverbial train.

5 Taming

Whip and tether guide the ox
preventing its fall to the wayward path.
Once properly trained,
the ox follows your way, untethered.

The tight rein that has kept both Ox and mind in check can now be loosened (but not discarded), for both have been tamed. The time for wrestling is over, and we become more confident in and accustomed to the practice. However, the rope must not be dropped, because then there would be the conviction that we are in total control, with no need to concentrate in order to maintain our guard, a dangerous assumption.

6 Riding home

You wend your way home, astride the ox.
The rustic flute chimes with the crimson evening mist.
With joy unbounded, you sing and play.
For these sounds transcend the human heart.

The rope is now redundant, for the Ox knows its way home. Nevertheless, both Ox and Ox-herd remain separate entities. It is inappropriate to replace the symbolism of Ox and rider with that of the *centaur*,[3] not two distinct creatures but one, bereft of dualities. As the practice is no longer seen as a challenge, music and laughter bubble from within us. As the tension abates, our minds are freed and there is much room for creativity.

7　The Ox is forgotten

Having ridden it home,
the ox is no more in mind.
Under the high red sun you daydream.
There is no place for whip or tether.

As surely as the Ox and the Ox-herd have, until now, been regarded as separate entities, so has the practitioner regarded the practice as something other than himself. But now there is no Ox in mind and no duality in meditation. Practice is no longer something restricted to certain times of the day that have no bearing on the rest of the time. Instead, it becomes a way of life for us as we set about our chores and routine.

8 And so is the Ox-herd

All is empty, you, the ox, the whip, the tether.
No mind can comprehend the vastness of heaven.
Can the roar of the furnace sustain one flake of snow?
Having reached this state, you are at one with the way.

Although there is a need to undergo Zen training, the objective is not a trained Ox; the ultimate goal is not recognition of the supremacy of the Ox-herd over a wayward creature (man's mind). Nor is the symbolism of the *centaur* appropriate, for both metaphors have now been transcended. The void of the circle reminds us that we, too, are empty; empty in the sense that we can never be independent entities in our own right. Nor are we (or anything else for that matter) here forever. Rather, we are but fleeting moments crossing the ocean of transformation. This is not the closed door of despair, but the window open to opportunity. No longer do we have to strive to cling to that which we fear may desert us; we can but care for whatever is on loan to us for as long as it lasts. But nothing lasts forever, not even us. To know this is the great release, the window to our Buddha-nature; practice and practitioner are now one.

9 Back to the source

You return to the source, the effort over.
Now you feel blind and deaf.
You see nothing outside, not even the birds,
though the flames are red, the waters boundless.

Having recognized that all is emptiness, we must let that go also, not clinging even to that earth-shattering knowledge. Although everything is empty, we, too, are part of that emptiness, and the window to our Buddha-nature remains shuttered unless we open the door to the world. The realization that we *are* the world removes the last remnants of duality, and the last of our fears, for how can we fear ourselves? All of life is on our doorstep, and it took our practice to make us see it.

10 Entering the marketplace with giving hands

Ragged and bare-footed, you enter the marketplace,
covered in mud and dust yet smiling broadly.
Needing not the power of gods,
You bring even the withered trees to bloom.

The final stage finds us completely at one with the world. The ragged, pot-bellied man who enters the marketplace has no concern for appearances, so he enters bare-footed. He does carry a bag, but its contents weigh far more than any material possessions; instead, he brings wisdom, compassion and loving kindness in abundance. Accordingly, he is equally at home anywhere in the world, recognizing that monasteries and "high places" do not have a monopoly on spirituality. With the ego now stilled (it will always be there), gone is the creator of duality, no more the author of discrimination. Instead, we love others as much as we love ourselves, and help them accordingly. It is now meaningless to think of others as being very different to ourselves; hence, duality, deceit and ill-will become things of the past.

The Ten Ox-herding Pictures do not symbolize linear progression, since we constantly backslide. We bring to Zen the habits of a lifetime, many of which, because of our prejudices, mitigate against meaningful meditation. We must not fear when we disappoint ourselves and others, for we are constantly deepening our understanding as we continue to practise.

2 Zen Roots

This shall ye think of
All this fleeting world;
A star at dawn;
A bubble in a stream;
A flash of lightning in a summer cloud;
A phantom in a dream.
Diamond sutra

Among the names of those notables from the Land of the Rising Sun credited with the bringing of Zen Buddhism to the West are to be found Soen Roshi and Nyogen Sensaki. However, the one name that shines forth like a beacon is Daisetz Teitaro Suzuki. Nineteenth-century Romanticists such as Schelling and Carus displayed an interest in the transcendental that beseeched enquiry into the philosophical speculations of the Oriental mind. This paved the way for Japanese apologists such as Suzuki, who were steeped in nationalistic tendencies yet, at the same time, fascinated with western culture. The high-minded words of these worthies soon found favour with western scholars who, in their anxiety to learn from the eastern mind, accepted their views uncritically. Oriental scholars, meanwhile, were equally anxious that Zen Buddhism should be made comprehensible to the western reader, and this prompted Suzuki, for one, to introduce Zen within a formula propounded by William James of the American School of the Psychology of Religion.

I have said already that D. T. Suzuki was probably the greatest single influence in bringing Zen Buddhism to the West. Suzuki presented Zen to the West as pure mysticism, beyond human reason and understanding, beyond metaphysics and philosophy, and outside the remit of any historical or religious framework. There developed in the minds of some writers the popular misconception that "Zen Buddhism" and "Buddhism" were somehow different, strange bedfellows with no common heritage. Accordingly, Zen drew its first breath in the West not as a child of Buddhism, but as an orphan, rejoicing in the name of "Pure Experience" and having no necessary blood ties with either culture or religion: "If there is anything Zen strongly emphasizes it is the attainment of freedom . . . Zen is a wafting cloud in the sky. No screw fastens it, no screw holds it; it moves as it lists."[1]

Clearly Suzuki had a point, and few would disagree that neither philosophical inquiry nor historical investigation can provide the complete answers to the Zen experience; no more can these systems explain the higher transcendental realms of any other religion. Equally clearly, any study which either ignores or evades the enormous influence that metaphysical speculation and historical analysis have had upon a religion cannot be considered a responsible one, and Suzuki's thesis has never really been accepted in scholarly circles. Accordingly, while acknowledging that the Zen experience transcends time and space, we will do well to remember the words of Rudolf Otto when he wrote of metaphysics, "no mysticism can exist purely in the blue; it invariably rests on a foundation which it mightily seeks to deny but which gives it a special character and an identity different from all other forms of mysticism".[2] Similarly, the responsible study is one that places Zen Buddhism in its historical context and critically examines the evidence accordingly.

The origin of the tradition that began with Sakyamuni, the Buddha Siddhartha Gautama, is of fundamental importance to Zen. Its veneration and appreciation find expression in the chanting of the names of each of the successive fifty-two patriarchs to whom it was transmitted over twenty-five centuries, as part of the daily service in traditional Zen monasteries. It is important to remember the source, for Zen has had to find expression within the culture within which it found itself. The singing of the scriptures in English to a plainsong chant would be but one of the many forms of expression with the Soto Zen tradition's adaptation to Western form.

The legacy of India

Neither the Buddha nor Buddhism appeared *one fine day* in a cultural vacuum, having no roots and no substance. Both are the offspring of India. That country is without equal as a nation whose spirit of acceptance of all that is new, and reluctance to discard that which is old, have typified the very heart of its people in their search for the highest spirituality, their quest for the Ultimate Reality. This is the essence of the Indian mind.

Some fifteen hundred years BCE, this same Indian mind, when confronted by nomadic Aryan tribes, long since departed from the Central Asian steppe, applied the same philosophy that it had employed since time immemorial, by absorbing the new into the old. The Aryan wanderer did not come alone nor, for that matter, on one occasion. In waves of settlement, sometime in the middle of the second millennium BCE, he began to enter the Indian subcontinent along a valley which later gave its name to the highly sophisticated civilization which was already in decline at the time of the Aryan invasions, the Indus Valley. With the Aryan came his herds of horses and cattle, his weavers, tanners, potters, carpenters and metal workers; with the Aryan came his social structure, and his religious belief systems.

An all too familiar picture at the end of the Late Bronze Age in the ancient East is one of settlement by a pastoral people who, by dint of conquest, deemed themselves to be intellectually and culturally superior to those they had vanquished, but in fact were directly responsible for reducing what was formerly a high level of civilization to a village culture. The Aryans were but one of numerous groups of Indo-European migrants who, over many centuries since the beginning of the second millennium BCE, had left their homeland for pastures new in both Europe and Asia; the group which entered India in the middle of the second millennium BCE may well have done so from Iran. This group was blind to the high degree of cultural sophistication enjoyed by the indigenous population, whom they called "barbarians". For their part, they rejoiced in the name *Arya*, emphasizing the "cultivated" or "noble" nuance of this term, rather than its true meaning, "agriculturalist".

The superiority they glowingly bestowed upon themselves did not manifest itself in literary achievements, however, for they were illiterate. As formulated as their religious belief systems may or may not have been, beliefs were handed down orally. The western mind has always regarded oral tradition as suspect, and very much the poor relation of the written word as far as accuracy of transmission is concerned; the eastern mind has no such delusions. Nevertheless, we have to look for a record of what Aryan/Vedic religion was like in the second millennium BCE to the *Rg Veda*, the earliest of the four *Vedas*. This text not only survived a long period of oral transmission, but contains material which was long out of date by the time of the Aryan incursions, as well as material which post-dated the settlement; consequently, the record is not without its problems.

Throughout the ancient East, settled communities have always had one eye on their crops and one on their gods, looking to the latter to propitiate the former. Although the discovery of a terracotta female figurine may have no necessary connection with religion,[3] it seems likely that a profusion of these artefacts excavated from pre-Aryan times in the Indus Valley attests to the presence of a fertility cult centred around the Mother Goddess. Nomadic or semi-nomadic tribes, however, were less concerned with fertility than the elements that affected their herds and controlled their wanderings. Their social structures were normally patriarchal, their gods similarly male-oriented.

Unsurprisingly, the early concerns of the *Rg Veda* are not directed towards the fertility of the soil with its attendant Mother Goddess worship, but with nature. Although female deities are not without mention in the *Vedas*, none enjoys independent status and each is dependent upon her consort for her position. The male gods, on the other hand, are gods in their own right. These *Vedic* gods were looked to for the controlling influence they have on human existence. Hence Agni, the god of fire, is mentioned in almost a third of the hymns of the *Rg Veda*. Not only was Agni functional in providing heat and food, Agni alone had the capacity to consume the sacrificial offering, thereby transforming it from its gross state into a form (smoke) which was acceptable to the gods. Similarly, the natural elements of rain and thunder, wind and storm, each has its attendant deity that can be discerned at both the microcosmic (as the breeze which fans the flames in the domestic hearth) and the macrocosmic (as the raging whirlwind) levels.

There were also different levels at which the sacrificial ritual known as *yajna* could be perceived. Sacrifice could only be offered by the hereditary brahmin priesthood and tensions developed over the monopoly it held over *yajna*. The need for a multiplicity of gods also began to be called to question, and in later *Vedas* this is apparent. In *Rg Veda* 2:1 vv. 3–5, for instance, Agni is identified with all the gods:

Hero of Heroes, Agni! thou art Indra, thou art Visnu
of the Mighty Stride, adorable . . .
Agni, thou art King Varuna whose laws stand fast;
as Mitra, Wonder-Worker, thou must be implored.[4]

If Agni, in one of his manifestations, takes the form of a thunderbolt,
it is small wonder that he is identified with Indra, the greatest of the
Aryan gods, and lord of war and weather. Basham raises the interesting
question, "Was there only one Agni, or were there many Agnis? How
could Agni be one and many at the same time?"[5] It was questions like
these which perplexed the Aryan mind and led to the development of
monism, so prominent in *Upanisadic* teaching.

The vast multiplicity of gods which epitomized *Vedic* thought were
not autonomous, however; each was reponsible to the cosmic norm, *rta*,
the regulating force which was at the heart of the cosmos, the custodian
of which was Varuna. *Rta* was the regulating pulse which governed
manifest existence, both on the microcosmic and the macrocosmic
levels. *Rta* it was which gave the planets their orbits, caused the sun to
rise and set, the seasons to come and go, and nature to survive. It was
also *rta* which set the norms for social and moral behaviour. Those who
did not conform to these norms were answerable to Varuna, as were the
gods. The concept of *dharma* ("what is right"), which later became a
fundamental principle of Hinduism, had its birth pangs in *rta*.

The doubts which had begun to arise in the Aryan mind regarding
the individuality of the gods gained momentum, and by the time of *Rg
Veda* 2:1 Agni, long associated with Indra, was being identified with all
the gods. Also gaining momentum was the move towards monotheism.
If the identity of the gods was becoming indistinct, then there must be
a force behind the gods, but this force could not be *rta*! *Rta* was certainly
a force *par excellence*: equally certainly it was more fundamental than
any deity, but it was an impersonal force, a universal Law which had to
be upheld, rather than acting of its own volition.

In late *Vedic* literature, such as the *Brahmanas* and the *Aranyakas*,
the so-called forest writings, there are clear indications of the move
towards a more speculative and mystical approach to religion which
became crystallized at the end of the *Vedic* period known as *Vedanta*.
The literature of this period is known as the *Upanisads*, which means
"to sit down near", a reference to the close proximity to the *guru* of the
pupils or *chelas* who seated themselves at his feet. The teaching,
however, did not centre on the imparting of a corpus of knowledge, for
this was not the way of the *Upanisadic* sages; their thrust of thought

directed itself to evoking from their pupils the intuitive knowledge which is best described as "wisdom" which we all have, but exhibit all too infrequently.

Upanisadic literature represents the high watermark of the Indian mind, a mind which was forever searching for the Truth, the nature of the self, and of Ultimate Reality. Given this resolve, it is small wonder that these truths were not considered to be ones which could be taught or learned; they had to be *realized* at the deepest intuitive level of understanding. This level of understanding was entirely commensurate with the level of consciousness of the pupil at each stage of his development, and the thought-provoking questions of the *gurus* would be measured accordingly.

Upanisadic thought is anything but consistent; nevertheless, there is a common focus on the acceptance of a totally transcendent Absolute, a trend which arose in the *Vedic* period. This indescribable Absolute is called Brahman, which is incomprehensible to the human mind, but which nevertheless is the *Ground of all Being*, from which everything else emanates. The inevitable question to this theory is that anything which is incomprehensible to the human mind must, by definition, remain beyond humankind's understanding, so how can it be known? The *Upanisads* address this question by affirming that the Absolute, though Unmanifest, is directly linked to manifest existence through the innermost essence of each manifest entity – a permanent, unchanging essence called the *atman*. On this view, realization of the deepest intuitive knowledge or wisdom, which the *chelas* sought, meant realization of Brahman. This realization could only take place when the experience is bereft of subject and object, when the egoistic self has been overcome and the realization dawns that the true Self and Brahman are one and the same. Known as the Brahman: *atman* synthesis, this theory, which is central to *Upanisadic* thought, is the cornerstone of Indian philosophy. The Brahman: *atman* synthesis, which posits the theory of a permanent, unchanging self was anathema to Buddhists, and it was as a reaction to the synthesis that Buddhism first drew breath.

Certain orientalists in the West have regarded the Pali Canon as a systematized account of the Buddha's teaching, from which the development of Buddhist philosophy justifiably may be traced. Yet these discourses were never intended to be systematized; they are no more systematic than the thought-provoking dialogues of the *Upanisadic* sages of India, who worked patiently yet tirelessly to evoke the intuitive wisdom they knew lay sleeping within each and every one of their students. The development of Buddhist philosophy is to be found not

Zen Roots

in the Pali Canon, but in the tensions which grew up between *Upanisadic* and Buddhist thought as well as Buddhism's own internal differences.

The Life of the Buddha

The Buddha was born into an age of considerable social and political unrest, in the northern India of the sixth century BCE. It was a time when smaller tribes were being absorbed into larger monarchies and this brought about a period of insecurity that promoted a quest for personal identity, the purpose of life, and the meaning of ultimate truth and reality. Questions were being asked such as "What is the nature of eternity?", "What is real in a world of change?", "Why does humankind suffer?", and "What should we pursue as the spiritual goal of life?"

We have no one direct historical account of the Buddha's life. Instead we have various narratives which highlight different aspects of his life and teaching. The earliest accounts were not written until three or four hundred years after he lived, although some Buddhist scriptures were transmitted orally for several centuries from a time shortly after his *parinirvana*. The disciples and followers of the Buddha handed down their accounts of the Buddha's life and teaching, but often added their own thoughts and opinions; it is therefore difficult to abstract the historical events from the hagiographic nature of the material. These additions range from simple, brief descriptions to highly elaborated accounts occupying several volumes. Some accounts of the Buddha recount his descent from heaven, his miraculous deeds, his remarkable physical appearance and the like; other accounts refer to more metaphysical aspects, seeing the Buddha as a cosmic Buddha who comes to earth at a needy moment, being manifested in a series of existences in the world.

Like other Indian religions, Buddhism accepts the doctrines of *karma* and *samsara* and the Buddha, too, is believed to have been reborn over an incalculable period of aeons, each aeon being an unthinkably long period of time. When the Buddha achieved Enlightenment he became omniscient and was thus able to view his past lives through all this vast period of time; he told his followers about his past life experiences. Many of these stories are recounted in what are called the *Jatakas*, one group of which relates, in particular, the lives of the Buddha in animal form.[6] Other sources describe his previous lives in human form and so we hear of his meeting, in one life, with a great enlightened sage, Dipankara; we read of his sacrifice of his own body to a weak and hungry tigress in another; and his loss of life as a Preacher of Patience in yet another. All these stories from past lives are said to have occurred in *cosmic* time, so called because they occurred in lives beyond the present *historical* time in which we live. The Buddha of *this* aeon, Siddhattha Gotama (Skt. Siddhartha Gautama), is thus the historical Buddha and is distinguished so by being called *Sakyamuni*, "the sage from the tribe of Sakyas".

Disentangling the hagiographical material from all these accounts, in an attempt to establish the true historical background, is a task undertaken not only by scholars in the West, but by eastern scholars within Buddhism also. Japanese scholars in particular have done thorough work in this field, but also notable for their efforts are the monks of Sri Lanka. The earliest sources have been scrutinized carefully in an attempt to disentangle fact from legend. There are four major accounts of the life of the Buddha. Three of these are written in Sanskrit: the *Mahavastu*, the *Lalitavistara* and the *Buddhacarita*. Another work, the *Nidanakatha*, is a Pali work – Pali being the language of the canonical scriptures of Theravada Buddhism,[7] the branch of Buddhism found in Sri Lanka, Burma, Thailand and Cambodia. The first complete biography of the Buddha is presented in the *Buddhacarita*, "The Acts of the Buddha", which was written in the first century CE by the poet Asvaghosa. The first thirteen cantos are extant in Sanskrit, the rest in the Tibetan translation.

It is a valuable account in that it is a complete one of the Buddha's life, and it is the one that I shall be relying on in particular for the events of his life. Dates for the life of the Buddha are uncertain and chronology for this period is accurate only within a decade. The conventionally accepted dates for the Buddha's life are 566–486 BCE, though Professor Gombrich has recently assigned the Buddha's death to the last decade of the fifth century BCE.[8]

The account of the Buddha's life in the *Buddhacarita* and other sources

The *Buddhacarita* tells us that Siddhartha was born into a family of the Sakya clan in the kingdom of Sakya (modern Nepal). Sakya was in north-east India in the foothills of the Himalayas, on the northern edge of the Ganges basin. He was born, so the account goes, into the *ksatriya* class, and the family's name was Gautama. His father was a *raja*, ruler of the Sakya kingdom, so Siddhartha Gautama, as he was called, was a prince living in a luxurious palace. Siddhartha is said to have been the personal name given to the prince by his father. It means "Aim-accomplished", but it occurs only in late texts and is unlikely to have been his original name. Indeed, Michael Pye makes the apt point that if we are "historically sober" we would have to say that we do not know what he would have been called by either family or friends.[9] Michael Carrithers observes that the Sakyas were one of a number of peoples domiciled in the then developing North Indian civilization whose systems of government are best described as "tribal republics", since they were ruled over by councils of elders or oligarchies. Certainly, some may have had leaders elected for a fixed term; equally certainly, these leaders were not kings, "and therefore the later tradition that the Buddha was a king's son must be dismissed".[10] However, to exclude all the traditions which are late, hagiographical and dubious would be to leave little left to discuss in the life of the Buddha and would do a disservice to Buddhist belief. We therefore need to examine the hagiographical accounts of the Buddha's life as much as the truly historical, if they are discernible.

Buddhist tradition relates that miraculous, portentous events are associated with his birth; for example, he was born out of his mother's side. It seems that all Buddhas are characterized by unusual births. The purpose of such a birth story is to portray the birth of an exceptional being and, indeed, the *Buddhacarita* certainly does this, for Siddhartha was born in full awareness, and was already in a high state of consciousness from the cumulative states of all his past lives. So, we are told, he walked immediately and is reputed to have said:

'I am born for supreme knowledge, for the welfare of the world, — thus, this is my last birth,' – thus did he of lion gait, gazing at the four quarters, utter a voice full of auspicious meaning.[11]

His mother died seven days after giving birth, for the womb that had borne a Buddha could not then carry another ordinary mortal. She was reborn in a celestial realm.

Traditionally, the people of the Sakya kingdom were somewhat independent and unorthodox in their thinking and nature, and were less likely to accept established traditions such as the rigid brahminism of Hinduism or the four-fold class system. The kingdom was an area that would produce other unorthodox thinkers besides the Buddha. The capital city of the area was Kapilavasta, and this would have been the place where Siddhartha was born. There is an inscription there today from ancient times stating "The Blessed One was born here". It would have been here in this capital that, according to the *Buddhacarita*, a forecast of the future enlightened life of Siddhartha was given to his father the *raja* by the sage Asita:

> He will proclaim the way of deliverance to those afflicted with sorrow, entangled in objects of sense, and lost in the forest paths of worldly existence, as to travellers who have lost their way.
>
> Book 1: 77

Alarmed by the sage's remarks, we are told that the *raja* imprisoned the growing boy within the boundaries of three palaces; one for the cold season, one for the rainy season and one for the hot season. He wanted his son to have a view of reality that was divorced from any concept of suffering or unhappiness. Without knowing of the natural state of humankind, he would not need to proclaim any path to something beyond it.

It was in these luxurious circumstances that Siddhartha grew up in a life of pure pleasure and indulgence, in which he married and had a son. This is an important aspect of the Buddhist tradition, perhaps important enough to have been embellished in the early sources to enhance its meaning. Characteristic of Hindu religion is the belief in *asramadharma*, the idea that each individual must pass through the four stages of life – celibate student, married householder, recluse and wandering mendicant. To achieve *moksa* and end the cycle of *samsara* it was believed to be necessary to experience all the *asramas*, though it was sometimes accepted that some could be born straight into the last *asrama*. Siddhartha's life reflects this pattern of *asramadharma* and his life in the palace is clearly the second *asrama*.[12] Moreover, the Buddha's eventual denial of the extremes of luxury and asceticism, which promoted a *Middle Way*, made this early period of luxurious and sensuous enjoyment an important one.

We can call Siddhartha at this stage a *bodhisattva*. This word is used in Buddhism in two senses. In Theravada Buddhism it means one who is on the way to enlightenment, but since Theravada Buddhism believes there can be only one Buddha in each aeon, there can be only one *bodhisattva* in this aeon, this historical time, and this would be Siddhartha when he was a Buddha-to-be. In Mahayana Buddhism the term *bodhisattva* was used, as it still is, to depict someone who has attained enlightenment (*bodhi*) but who has delayed final enlightenment, full *nirvana*, in order to stay in existence and help others to reach enlightenment too.

Despite his sheltered and luxurious life, we are told that Siddhartha heard about life outside the confines of the palaces and wished so much to experience the wider world. The *Buddhacarita* tells us:

> Having heard of the delightful appearance of the city groves beloved by the women, he resolved to go out of doors, like an elephant long shut up in a house.
>
> Book III: 3

Siddhartha pleaded with his father to be allowed outside his confined existence, and the *raja* agreed to allow his son beyond the palace up to a certain radius. All unpleasant sights, cripples, beggars and old people were hidden away, but it was to be Siddhartha's fate to experience what are now called the four signs. It is likely that these were illusions, some sources suggesting that they were engineered by the gods. Whatever Siddhartha's experiences were, it seems they were shared only by his chariot driver and it is likely that they were supernatural experiences. On his first journey from the palace, Siddhartha saw, for the first time in his life, an old man. The *Buddhacarita* tells of the immense and violent shock that this caused to the *bodhisattva*:

> Then he, the great-souled one, who had his mind purified by the impressions of former good actions, who possessed a store of merits accumulated through many preceding aeons, was deeply agitated when he heard of old age, like a bull who has heard the crash of a thunderbolt close by.
>
> Book III: 34

His following excursion brought the experience of a sick man and we are told that his reaction was one of despair. It is a depair filled also with amazement and sadness that the world is surrounded with old age and sickness and yet each individual seemed not to face it at all, but closed his or her eyes to it. The *Buddhacarita* tells us:

> Having heard this account, his mind deeply distressed, he trembled like the moon reflected in the waves of water; and full of sorrow he uttered these words in a low voice:
>
> 'Even while they see all this calamity of diseases mankind can yet feel tranquillity; alas for the scattered intelligence of men who can smile when still not free from the terror of disease!'
>
> Book III: 45– 46

It is the third vision of a corpse that brings the strongest reactions and which adds the final and very poignant experience of the nature of reality and life. Again, Siddhartha is amazed that humankind closes its eyes to this fact of death:

> Is this end appointed to all creatures, and yet the world throws off all fear and is infatuated! Hard indeed, I think, must the hearts of men be, who can be self-composed in such a road.
>
> Book III: 61

After these experiences, Siddhartha was a changed man. No longer could he view palace life as the norm of existence. All the things which normally attract the senses were no longer attractive to him; he saw them all as illusory:

> I do not despise worldly objects, I know that all mankind are bound up therein; but remembering that the world is transitory, my mind cannot find pleasure in them.
>
> Book IV: 85

This concept of the impermanence of all life and all the world was to be a very important one in Buddhism: because of the existence of old age, sickness and death, happiness, beauty and the many things which humankind clings to in life were seen by Siddhartha to be illusory and as things which should not be part of the life of the high-minded. He said:

> Real greatness is not to be found there, where there is universally destruction, or where there is attachment to earthly objects, or a want of self-control.
>
> Book IV: 91

A final excursion is depicted as a visit to the forest in search of peace. Here, again, Siddhartha was filled with pity and remorse. He saw the plough overturning the soil, the ploughmen suffering in the dust and the wind, the weary oxen, and the insects and tiny creatures that the plough had killed. This is the sense in which he sees all life as *dukkha*, unsatisfactory, suffering in the sense of the disharmony of all existence. As he reflected on his experiences he is reputed to have said:

> It is a miserable thing that mankind, though themselves powerless and subject to sickness, old age, and death, yet blinded by passion and ignorant, look with disgust on another who is afflicted by old age or diseased or dead.
>
> Book V: 12

Seeking solitude, Siddhartha gained his first insight into the three signs he had received:

> As he thus considered thoroughly these faults of sickness, old age, and death which belong to all living beings, all the joy which he had felt in the activity of his vigour, his youth and his life, vanished in a moment.
>
> He did not rejoice, he did not feel remorse; he suffered no hesitation, indolence, nor sleep; he felt no drawing towards the qualities of desire; he hated nor scorned another.
>
> Thus did this pure passionless meditation grow within the great souled-one . . .
>
> Book V 14– 16

While reflecting in this way, Siddhartha experienced his fourth illusion. This took the form of a mendicant, a homeless, wandering ascetic, someone on the fourth of the Hindu *asramas*. This marked the final turning point from his former life and he saw clearly, at that time, the *dharma* which he had to pursue. Accordingly, he decided to escape the palace in order to seek the state of deathlessness, to find the answers to the problems of old age, sickness and death in life. Siddhartha had experienced the disillusioning aspects of life, and he wished to seek liberation from them. What he had experienced was the predicament of humankind, the fact that (wo)man, placed in a temporal, materialistic existence, intoxicates him or herself with diversions, and ignores the materialistic realities of aging, suffering and death. Siddhartha saw this ignorance, and the ensuing indifference to the suffering of sentient beings in life, as immoral.

Asceticism and enlightenment

Bidding farewell to a stunned father, who upon receiving the news, "shook like a tree struck by an elephant", pleading with his son not to go, "in a voice choked with tears", Siddhartha summoned his faithful steed, Kamthaka, and prepared to forsake the palace. He had spent his youth and early manhood in extreme luxury: now he was to experience their very opposites in a life of total asceticism as a wandering recluse. He had come to realize the transience of all life and the necessity of transcending its suffering. In the *Buddhacarita* he is reported as telling Chandaka, his grieving groom:

Do not think of mourning for me who am thus gone forth from my home; union, however long it may last, in time will come to an end.

Since separation is certain, therefore is my mind fixed on liberation; how shall there not be repeated severings from one's kindred?

Do not think of mourning for me who am gone forth to leave sorrow behind; it is the thralls of passion, who are attached to desires, the causes of sorrow, for whom thou shouldst mourn.

Book VI: 16– 18

For Siddhartha, the world became an illusion in which people chased happiness in things that were impermanent. Material existence could not possibly be Reality, for Reality must be deathless. And so he tried to find the deathless state through extreme asceticism. For six years he became the most devoted of ascetics, eventually reducing his daily intake of food to one grain of rice. His wasted body is vividly described by Michael Pye:

Gradually he reduced himself to little more than skin and bone, his ribs protruded and his eyes in their hollowed sockets were little more than the sparkle of water at the bottom of deep wells. It is said that he could feel his spine through his stomach. When he moved from his position he fell from weakness and when he touched his discoloured limbs the hairs fell from their pores.[13]

The *Buddhacarita* tells us:

Having only skin and bone remaining, with his fat, flesh and blood entirely wasted, yet, though diminished, he shone with undiminished grandeur like the ocean.

Book XII: 96

Although he is admired by five companion Hindu monks who accompany him at the time, Siddhartha comes to realize that he is nowhere near finding the answers he seeks in life by the yoga of the ascetic. He thus reflects:

"This is not the way to passionlessness, nor to perfect knowledge, nor to liberation; that was certainly the true way which I found at the root of the Gambu tree."

"But that cannot be attained by one who has lost his strength," – so resuming his care for his body, he next pondered thus, how best to increase his bodily vigour.

Book XII: 98– 99

And so Siddhartha came to reject the ascetic path to enlightenment. Having regained his physical strength, he left his companions and journeyed to the holy town of Gaya, situated on a tributary of the Ganges. There, Siddhartha sat down under the shade of a great pipal tree and made a vow:

> I will not rise from this position on the earth until I have obtained my utmost aim.
>
> Book XII: 97

So he vowed to stay in that spot until he achieved enlightenment. He sat very quietly, very still, in the lotus *asana*, and began to go through the traditional *dhyanas* of meditation, gradually allowing his thoughts to subside until no new thoughts arose, and a feeling of joyful elation, coherence and tranquillity remained. At the final stages, a state of perfect balance, perfect equanimity was achieved. It was an equanimity which allowed him to reach back through all time and thus through previous lives; it was the point at which *karma* is nullified. Although completely aware of his surroundings, Siddhartha was unaffected by them. His mind was free to travel in any direction and to any part of human experience past, present and future but without any conditioned emotion.

But the path to enlightenment was not completely smooth. The *Buddhacarita* tells us that Siddhartha experienced the temptation of Mara, the foe of all *dharma*. The foe of *dharma* is desire and aversion. Mara began his attack on Siddhartha by sending all his forces against the *bodhisattva*. But Siddhartha pointed his right hand down to the earth to ask the earth to witness his meritorious acts of past existences and his right to pursue the goal of enlightenment at this point. The earth responded with such an earthquake that the demons of Mara fled in haste from the scene. So Mara tried more subtle tactics and sent his daughters Discontent, Delight and Thirst, and his three sons Flurry, Gaiety and Sullen Pride to deter the *bodhisattva's* quest. But they were defeated by the equanimity of the mind of Siddhartha. The tempting of Siddhartha here represents allegorically the subtle enemies of the mind, and the ego which prevent the individual from gaining freedom from *samsara*.

And so Siddhartha proceeded through the stages of meditation to the point of enlightenment. He perceived all his former births and his previous lives. He is said to have recalled a hundred thousand of his lives and all the pleasures and pains of each of them. He saw clearly the long thread which had brought him through countless generations to the present moment, and came to the conclusion that all that we view as real in the world is totally insubstantial. He now had *deva*-vision and could see and understand all the inhabitants of the cosmos and all the *karmic* forces which made up their happiness and sadness, evil and good, beauty and ugliness, and so on. But he himself was neither this nor that, beyond all such dualities. He was free: he had a knowledge of all that was to be known, free of the sense-pleasures, free of becoming and free of the ignorance which causes the individual to be reborn. As Pye says:

the great journey which he had pursued through so many existences had reached its end, all that was to be done had been done.[14]

Siddhartha had reached the state of *anatman* or 'no self', 'non-ego', and had realized *nirvana*. The *Buddhacarita* tells us that:

From the summit of the world downwards he could detect no self anywhere. Like the fire, when its fuel is burnt up, he became tranquil. He had reached perfection, and he thought to himself: "This is the authentic Way on which in the past so many great seers, who also knew all higher and lower things, have travelled on to ultimate and real truth. And now I have obtained it".[15]

It is worth remembering that neither the *Buddhacarita* here, nor any other text for that matter, equates the extinguishing of a flame with *nirvana*, a point missed by many, but drawn to our attention by Walpola Rahula:

An Arahant after his death is often compared to a fire gone out when the supply of wood is over, or to the flame of a lamp gone out when the wick and oil are finished. Here it should be clearly and distinctly understood, without any confusion, that what is compared to a flame or a fire gone out is not Nirvana, but the "being" composed of the Five Aggregates who realized Nirvana. This point has to be emphasized because many people, even some great scholars, have misunderstood and misinterpreted this simili as referring to Nirvana. Nirvana is never compared to a fire or a lamp gone out.[16]

As the dawn broke, Siddhartha became the Buddha, the Awakened One:

Thus he, the holy one, sitting there on his seat of grass at the root of the tree, pondering by his own efforts attained at last perfect knowledge.

Then bursting the shell of ignorance, having gained all the various kinds of perfect intuition, he attained all the partial knowledge of alternatives which is included in perfect knowledge.

Zen Roots

He became the perfectly wise, the Bhagavat, the Arhat, the king of the Law, the Tathagata, He who has attained the knowledge of all forms, the Lord of all science.

Book XIV: 66– 68

At that moment, sources tell us that the blind could see, the deaf could hear, and the lame could walk; there was beauty and peace in all the world:

Pleasant breezes blew softly, rain fell from a cloudless sky, flowers and fruits dropped from trees out of season – in an effort as it were, to show reverence for him. Mandarava flowers and lotus blossoms, and also water lilies made of gold and beryl, fell from the sky on the ground near the Shakya sage, so that it looked like a place in the world of the gods. At that moment no one anywhere was angry, ill or sad; no one did evil, none was proud; the world became quite quiet, as though it had reached full perfection.[17]

Clearly, Siddhartha had transcended the apparent limits of human perception, but human curiosity, being what it is, will forever ask, "But what happened precisely?", a concern addressed rather well by Andrew Powell:

The Buddha's Enlightenment is the central fact of the Buddhist religion. It is as fundamental as the Crucifixion is to Christianity. The great edifice of Buddhist philosophy and ethics which developed in succeeding centuries could never have been constructed without this one crucial occurrence. So what exactly happened? What is Enlightenment? Unfortunately it is rather difficult to say because it is an experience, one which cannot readily be reduced to the conventional formulas of language. If it could be easily explained, then it would no longer be Enlightenment.[18]

Coming out of his long seven-day trance into full Enlightenment, the sources inform us that Mara again tempted the Buddha to reject the world and enter final *nirvana, parinirvana*. But it is at the request of the two Hindu gods, Indra and Brahma, that the Buddha decides to remain in the world to guide others on the path and teach them the true *dharma*. The story is a strange one, perhaps reflecting allegorically some uncertainty in the Buddha as to how, practically, he could put humankind on this true *dharmic* path. Perhaps this is what the conflicting ideas of the appearance of Mara and the deities represent.

So the Buddha did not pass into final *parinirvana* but completed the remainder of his life in his physical body without producing any more *karma* which would cause him to be reborn. His purpose now would be to teach the *dharma* and in making this decision there was evident a radical shift from the individualistic and elitist striving for *moksa* of brahmanical Hinduism; it was a turning towards the hosts of humanity (with the possible exception of women!) regardless of class. When once again the Buddha was reunited with his father, the latter was able to recognize the new role of his son, and accept also that Siddhartha's decisions had been the right ones. He said:

> If you had chosen to remain bound up with the things of this world, you could as a universal monarch have protected mankind. Instead you have conquered the great ills of the Samsaric world, you have become a Sage who proclaims the Dharma for the weal of all. [19]

Importantly, there is no indication of any involvement with a transcendent Absolute or theistic concept of the divine during the process in which the Buddha achieved Enlightenment. Similarly, when the Buddha reached his goal there was no sense of unity with, either partially or wholly, a transcendent Absolute. The gods seem to have helped Siddhartha towards Enlightenment, and he is depicted as visiting them in their heaven to give them spiritual calm and teaching. The gods of Buddhism are *karmic*; they are only there because they have accumulated immense amounts of good *karma*. But because they have *karma* they are inferior to the Buddha, and are still fellow travellers with all humanity on the *samsaric* path. So Enlightenment for the Buddha brought him superiority to these gods and not knowledge of an Absolute. When asked who taught him Enlightenment, the Buddha replied:

> No teacher have I. None need I venerate, and none must I despise. Nirvana have I now obtained, and I am not the same as others are. Quite by myself, you see, have I the Dharma won. Completely have I understood what must be understood, though others failed to understand it. That is the reason why I am a Buddha. [20]

We can gather from the various sources that, for the next forty or forty-five years of his life, the Buddha travelled in the middle Ganges region as a religious wandering monk, teaching and gathering disciples. He would have been considered as a *sannyasin*, a holy man, and would have been treated with respect and reverence, as all such holy men in the Indian tradition. Finally, some time towards the end of the fifth century BCE, the Buddha felt his death approaching, and he passed away, the victim of food poisoning. As a *tathagata*, one who is fully awakened and is in a state of "suchness" or "thusness", the Buddha could have continued living until the end of the present aeon, the accounts inform us, but he relinquished this right to live longer. The realization that the Buddha was about to die was too much for his devoted disciple, Ananda, and the old man was reduced to tears. The Buddha told him:

> do not mourn, do not weep. Haven't I told you that we are separated, parted, cut off from everything dear and beloved? . . . You have served me long with love, helpfully, gladly, sincerely and without reserve, in body, word, and thought. You have done well by yourself, Ananda. Keep trying and you will soon be liberated.[21]

Tradition states that one morning, the Buddha gathered alms at Vaisali, gave the town one last "elephant look" and then set his face towards Kusinagasa, quite near to his birthplace. There, surrounded by his disciples and local inhabitants, he entered into the stages of meditation and finally relinquished his body. No residue of *karmic* forces – negative or positive – remained that could bring about another birth. The Buddha was dead.

3 Doctrines Germane to Zen

According to Buddhism, whatever exists is a stream of becoming; nothing that exists is permanent. A beautiful but fragile blossom best exemplifies the Buddhist view of existence, for beautiful as it may be, it is clearly a passing phenomenon, as all who have seen the wind and rain driving newly opened cherry blossoms to the ground know very well. For one who thinks that these blossoms should be permanent this may seem tragic, but for someone who understands that change – the continuous rising and falling of existence – is the very nature of existence, the joy of seeing the beautiful blossoms is not destroyed by their falling. Only when this vast stream of becoming is mistaken for a conglomeration of *permanent things,* subject to various modifications, but nonetheless unchanging at their very core, does change threaten to destroy existence.[1]

B asic, original doctrines, fundamental to Zen Buddhism, are replete in the teachings of the Buddha. I have said already that the origin of the tradition that began with Sakyamuni is of primary importance to Zen. Once the Buddha had achieved Enlightenment, he began to attract a number of followers. This was the beginning of the *Sangha,* the community of monks,[2] though it is doubtful if the Buddha had any idea how it would develop when he discharged his disciples with the words:

Go monks and travel for the welfare and happiness of the people, out of compassion for the world . . .

Vin 1:21

To become ordained it was normally accepted that a man (not a woman at first) should become an *arahant*, a perfected one who had reached the egoless state of *nirvana*. Having reached this state of perfection, the shaving of the head and beard followed, as did the wearing of yellow rags and abandonment of the home. Once ordained, these *arahants* were sent out by the Buddha to teach the *dharma* and, as the *Sangha* grew in size, it became necessary for these ordained monks to ordain others rather than have everyone travel long distances for ordination by the Buddha himself. Soon, the process of ordination became fixed with the pattern of the candidate shaving hair and beard, putting on the yellow robe, squatting down before the monks with palms together in salutation, and reciting the three refuges three times:

I go to the Buddha for refuge
I go to the *Dharma* for refuge
I go to the *Sangha* for refuge

This basic, original formula is cited frequently in Zen Buddhism today, both before and after teaching sessions, as well as in ceremomies and on other occasions.[3]

The *dharma* of the Buddha

The word *dhamma* (Pali) *dharma* (Skt.) has different meanings in Indian thought: here it is used in the sense of "right" as opposed to "wrong". The basic teachings of the Buddha are the *dharmas*, the right ways or teachings about life. Indeed, Buddhists in Asia do not use the term "Buddhism", preferring to speak of the *dharma* of the Buddha. Before the Buddha's first teaching and after his Enlightenment, he drew a wheel on the ground. This symbolized the starting of the wheel of order, law or *dharma*, the wheel being an ancient Indian symbol. After drawing attention to the wheel of *dharma*, the Buddha expounded the importance of realizing the need for *dharma*. He taught the Four Noble Truths.

The Indian mind has long been tormented by the problem of *dukkha*, the realization that mankind will have to endure the suffering experienced not just in one lifetime, but in virtually countless lifetimes, some eighty-three thousand million lifetimes according to Hindu thought. This treadmill was seen by Indian philosophers as an "aimless wandering" through eternity, a continuous cycle of death and rebirth, repeated *ad infinitum*, appropriately termed *samsara*, "that which turns around forever". It was to the problem of suffering that the Buddha turned his attention. He urged his monks not to waste their time and energy speculating over metaphysical and philosophical problems such as how the world began, and how it would end; instead, they should direct their attention to the arising and cessation of suffering within their own being.

Because the Buddha recognized the problem, identified the cause of the problem, affirmed that there is a cure, and prescribed a remedy, it comes as no great surprise to find that his *dharma* is often compared to that of a medical practitioner, who writes a prescription for treating the human condition. This is why the Buddha is known as "the Great Physician". In his very first sermon in the Deer Park at Isipatana the Buddha set out the kernel of his *dharma*, as found in the Four Noble Truths. In the original texts these Four Truths are prescribed, appropriately *in capsule form*, though there are many other early texts which expound the teachings thoroughly and frequently in a variety of ways. The Four Noble Truths are:

1 *Dukkha*
2 *Samudaya*, the root cause of *dukkha*
3 *Nirodha*, the end of *dukkha*
4 *Magga*, the way to end *dukkha*

The First Noble Truth: *dukkha*

Although tensions exist between *Upanisadic* and Buddhist thought, the problem of suffering *(dukkha)* is a common concern, the running sore of Indian philosophy. In both philosophical belief systems, release from suffering is accompanied by release from bondage and hence escape from the *samsaric* cycle, the attainment of *moksa* (Hinduism) or *nirvana* (Buddhism). Of the two, the *Upanisads* depict this ideal state in the more positive terms, describing it as "consciousness" or "bliss". For the Buddhist, however, realization of *nirvana* is described in negative terms, to be achieved by the annihilation of sorrow, the blowing out of the three defilements of desire/greed, hatred/anger, and delusion.

> Anyone can become angry – that is easy. But to be angry with the right person, to the right degree, at the right time, for the right purpose, and in the right way – that is not easy.
>
> Aristotle, *The Nicomachean Ethics*

Both philosophical systems agree that this ultimate state is beyond description, for this would reduce it to the level of human understanding. The ultimate, however, is beyond comprehension, beyond experience, beyond language. But it is not beyond belief, any more than the person who has never experienced, and is quite incapable of describing, perfect health would deny that such a state exists. Both systems are also of one accord regarding the attainment of the Ultimate:

> Both have to speak of the ultimate as devoid of empirical determinations, as incomparable to anything we know; silence is their most proper language. They also agree that no empirical means, organisational device, sacrifice or penance, can bring us to the goal. Only insight into the nature of the real can avail.[4]

It is here that the tensions between the two systems become manifest, however, to such an extent that they part company, for what is real to one is anathema to the other. For the *Upanisadic* sages, the real is the Self, is *atman*, is Brahman. It is the attachments to and associations with the Self's appurtenances in manifest existence that spin a web of deceit, delusion and unreality, placing limits upon that which is real and beyond limitation. In this light, it is clear that the Ultimate Reality, the Self/Brahman/*atman*, call it what you will, is beyond description, *neti neti* "not this, not that", beyond the senses and beyond human perception.

Accordingly, the reality of the *Upanisads* is not one of empirical knowledge, wherein the seers expound all they know of Brahman before a receptive audience. On the contrary, their starting point is an intuitive knowledge, over which they do not hold the exclusive rights. Theirs was the way not of expounding upon, but of drawing out, provoking the student into drawing on the wisdom which is inherent, though dormant, within us all. The *Upanisads* are unequivocal that bondage to the *samsaric* cycle is due entirely to ignorance *(avidya)*, the ignorance of knowledge of the Self. Realization of the Self *(atmakama)* in *Upanisadic* thought is the fulfilment of *(aptakama)* and hence the transcendence of *(akama)*, all desires; this is the sole means of overcoming the ignorance which binds mankind to the *samsaric* wheel of bondage.

To the Buddhist, however, any talk of an *atman* or permanent, unchanging Self, the very kernel of *Upanisadic* thought, is anathema, a false notion of manifest proportion. For the Buddha, what masquerades as a person is in fact no more than a bundle of five dynamic constituents. Notwithstanding the fact that the Buddha's *dharma* centred upon the problem of suffering, to give *dukkha* such a limited interpretation and conclude that the First Noble Truth's affirmation is "all life is suffering", is to misrepresent the Buddha's *dharma.*

Let it be said that the prominent feature of Buddhism is neither pessimism nor, for that matter, optimism, but realism. It is realistic in the sense that it sees the world for what it is and mankind for what it is, with no promises of rewards and threats of punishments from a Creator God who is all-knowing and all-seeing, an omnipotent God who resides "somewhere up there" who created us imperfectly, yet for reasons best known to himself punishes us for our imperfections (or at very least does nothing to alleviate them). The reality of the situation, according to the Buddha's *dharma*, is that man is the author of his own destiny.

The Pali word *dukkha* is used as the direct opposite of *sukha*, which means being at "ease" in the sense of being happy or comfortable. It is therefore tempting to translate *dukkha* as "dis-ease" or "unsatisfactory", a comment on the ills of the world, the disharmony manifest in human existence. Although in common parlance, *dukkha* is undoubtedly used to convey the meaning of "suffering" in the sense of being in "pain" or "misery", it also has the nuance of "imperfection", "impermanence" or "emptiness". Rather than baldly translate *dukkha* as "suffering", and thereby misrepresent its many nuances in the First Noble Truth, following Rahula, I will leave the Pali word untranslated.[5]

The acceptance that *dukkha* permeates the whole of existence is not to affirm that there can be no place for happiness. Indeed, the many different forms happiness can take are clearly set out in the *Anguttara-nikaya*, while in the *Majjhima-nikaya* (both these early Pali texts contain original collections of the Buddha's discourses) the Buddha praises the blissful equanimity experienced in the high spiritual state of *dhyana*. However, all these states of happiness, which include physical and mental happiness, as well as the joy experienced in family life, sense pleasures and even *dhyana*, have one thing in common – impermanence. It is this common factor, especially the failure to recognize this commonality, which makes all things *dukkha*. Buddhism is a belief system which regards reality as a process, a state of flux; unsurprisingly, this is known as Process Philosophy. For Buddhists, there is no such thing as a state of unchanging permanence: the real is never being, but forever in the process of coming to be, or becoming.

It has been said already that Buddhism is neither pessimistic nor optimistic but realistic. The realism of the Buddha's *dharma* is conspicuous in his advice on happiness. Liberation from *dukkha* may be achieved only by the acceptance that all happiness is impermanent. Even within a loving family enriched with caring parents and happy children this happiness is not meant to be permanent; efforts to artificially enforce this supposed permanence will produce only unhappiness. In any event, even to talk of a permanent relationship is linguistic nonsense; since, according to the Buddha's teaching, no person can be considered to be a permanent entity, there can be no such thing as a permanent relationship. Whilst it is perfectly acceptable to enjoy any relationship while it lasts, to regard this relationship as immutable and thereby form permanent attachment is folly. Failure to recognize this basic fact can only induce heartache and suffering, yet day after day we continue to live our lives as if we will walk this planet at least for a couple of centuries, if not for all eternity![6] The *dukkha* produced with the realization that our happiest moments are precisely that – moments and no more – as well as the everyday suffering we encounter from unpleasant persons, conditions, or the like, are well known to us, and require no explanation. But there is another form of *dukkha*, known as *samkhara-dukkha*, which requires our attention. What in common language is spoken of as a "person", an "individual", or simply "I" or "me", was never viewed by the Buddha in the same light as non-Buddhists see it. For the Buddha, any being is not a permanent, unchanging self, but simply a combination of five aggregates or *kkhandhas* (Skt. *skandhas*); it is these five aggregates which *are dukkha*.

The five aggregates

> I am a frog swimming happily in the clear water of a pond
> And I am the grass-snake that silently feeds itself on the frog.
> I am the child in Uganda, all skin and bone, my legs as thin as
> bamboo sticks.
> And I am the arms merchant selling deadly weapons to Uganda.
>
> I am the twelve-year-old girl, refugee on a small boat,
> who throws herself into the ocean after being raped by a sea pirate.
> And I am the pirate, my heart is not yet capable of seeing and loving.
>
> *Please Call Me by My True Names*
>
> by Thich Nhat Hanh

The Buddha's statement that, contrary to popular belief, an individual has no permanent self or soul, but is really no more than a combination of five factors which are in a state of constant flux, is, by definition, an affirmation that the five factors of so-called individuality *are* suffering. Since these constituents which comprise what we normally call a "being" are constantly shifting, inevitably suffering will permeate every being's life at some time or other. The five aggregates are:

The Aggregate of Matter

The whole of matter is included here, including our five sense organs and the identifiable features recognized by our sense organs, such as those things that may be identified through being visible or audible. Also included are some of those thoughts and ideas that are about matter.

The Aggregate of Feelings or Sensations

that may be pleasant, unpleasant or neutral. The hair standing on the back of one's neck together with a cold chill down one's spine would be examples of the second aggregate.

The Aggregate of Perceptions

that recognize, identify and interpret the sensations experienced by our senses. In the above example it is this aggregate which would recognize the sensations in question as symptoms of fear.

The Aggregate of Mental Formations

Time and again the Buddha stressed that *karma* can be produced only through volition. In other words the action must be intentional. In this *karma*-producing aggregate fifty-two volitional activities including hate and desire, wisdom and ignorance are to be found; also included is the fallacious idea of a self or *atman*.

The Aggregate of Consciousness

This last aggregate is entirely dependent upon the previous four aggregates and does not constitute the equivalent of a self or soul.

Central to an understanding of the First Noble Truth is the realization that there is no more to (wo)man than the five attachment groups known as the five *skandhas*, and that these five groups are in a state of constant flux. In the course of this flux suffering must inevitably arise; therefore the five attachment groups are *dukkha*. This is really a doctrine of no *soul* rather than a doctrine of no *self*. As Michael Pye states:

there is no central organising principle apart from these, which could be thought of as independent of them and which might have some spiritual destiny of its own. Thus the Buddha taught that there is no such thing as a disembodied soul, or for that matter a soul beyond our ordinarily constituted consciousness.[7]

The self is totally impermanent and in attempting to make things permanent suffering occurs. The five constituents are always changing and are never the same from one moment to the next. They continually create *karmic* forces that will re-group after the person has died; having created the forces the person must be reborn to experience the results. The Buddhist, therefore, has to put aside the concept of "I" and "mine" in order to be free from suffering. Edward Conze puts it very simply:

> Here is the idea of "I", a mere figment of the imagination, with nothing real to correspond to it. There are all sorts of processes going on in the world. Now I conjure up another figment of the imagination, the idea of "belonging", and come to the conclusion that some, not particularly well defined portion of this world "belongs" to that "I" or to "me".[8]

So individuality has to be eliminated by ridding oneself of the belief in it. Conze further states:

> The insertion of a fictitious self into the actuality of our experience can be recognised wherever I assume that anything is mine, or that I am anything, or that anything is myself.[9]

Only through wisdom can we eliminate individuality. Wisdom involves the knowledge of impermanence – that everything is in a state of change, nothing ever becomes for everything is always becoming; of no-self in that there is no permanent unchanging "I" apart from the *skandhas*; and the knowledge that all life is *dukkha*, and the reason for this.

The Second Noble Truth: *samudaya*, the origin of *dukkha*

Recognition that suffering is caused, rather than just happening, is one of the hallmarks of the Buddha's greatness. For him, this was beyond question; indeed, it is the second of the Four Noble Truths. Having made this diagnosis, the Great Physician set about writing the prescription. The Buddha was unequivocal that once the factors upon which suffering is dependent are removed, suffering will cease.

To this end, and in keeping with the Indian concept of life as cyclical, Buddhists have designed what is generally known as the Wheel of Becoming *(bhavacakra)*. This is really a pictorial representation of the theory of dependent origination when applied to those processes which are said to make up what is normally described as the self. As the name implies, it represents the notion that *there are no beings, only becomings* in diagrammatic form. The three driving forces of ignorance, greed, and aversion are depicted at the hub of the wheel and are represented by a pig, a cockerel and a snake, each linked together, each biting the other's tail. The hub is surrounded by a circle with a black and a white half, depicting the *karmic* movement of beings ascending to a higher state and descending to a lower existence. Notwithstanding their denial that there are any clear-cut divisions between the processes which constitute a person, Buddhists have isolated an arbitrary twelve factors, in their efforts to demonstrate the causes of suffering.

If we start with *ignorance,* which is generally taken as the root cause of suffering (still bearing in mind that we are viewing a continuous process with no beginning and no end), the twelve factors may be listed as:

1 Ignorance
2 Impulses to action
3 Consciousness
4 Body and Mind
5 Six senses
6 Sense impressions
7 Perception
8 Desire
9 Grasping
10 Becoming
11 Birth
12 Old age and Death

Each of the twelve factors on the *bhavacakra* is generated by the preceeding factor,

> . . . the arising and the falling of the various factors of existence constitutes the unending continuum of process that makes up reality. Human beings are caught up in this cycle, being born, suffering and dying; being

born, suffering and dying, time after time. Life brings death and death brings life, as these are no more than phases in the eternal process.[10]

For the Buddhist, removal of the factors which cause suffering will bring about the elimination of suffering, but it is important to realize that the Buddha did not advocate nihilism. In other words, he did not teach that the elimination of suffering could only be achieved by the annihilation of life.

In order to appreciate what the Buddha did mean, we have to return to his teaching on the five *skandhas*, the dynamic bundle of constituents which make up a person, what most people would call the "self". The Buddha did not teach that there is no such thing as the self, but that there is no permanent, unchanging self; in other words there is nothing which could be said to constitute a self beyond the five *skandhas* – this is the theory of *anatta*. The "ignorance" referred to on the Wheel of Becoming is the delusion that as well as the five *skandhas* which constitute a person, within each person there also exists a self.

In this light, it is clear why ignorance is said to be the root cause of suffering. The delusion that a self exists beyond the five *skandhas* gives rise to the desires and aversions that this self experiences. It is then a short step to form attachments to this self, and so the suffering continues. In Buddhist eyes, living a life under the delusion that we all have a self in addition to the five *skandhas* is living a lie, and it is this lie which has to be annihilated, not life itself. Clearly, this teaching has nothing to do with nihilism. Accordingly, when we speak in terms of preventing "Birth" on the Wheel of Becoming in order to break the cycle and thereby negate suffering, the birth to which we refer is not life itself, but the birth of the ego. This is the key to the end of suffering.

Dependent Origination

Furthermore, there can be no belief in a first cause in Buddhism since everything is said to depend upon something else; this cyclical concept is known as Dependent Origination, Conditioned Genesis, or *paticca-samuppada*. This concept is one of the cornerstones of Buddhist philosophy, and was acknowledged as such by Sakyamuni:

> Oh Monks, one who understands this doctrine of dependent origination understands the Dharma; one who understands the Dharma, understands this doctrine of dependent origination.

Since this principle holds that everything in existence depends upon something else, then any talk of linear causality becomes vacuous, causality must be cyclical. This thesis is discernible in the life-cycle of the apple. The apple depends for its creation upon the blossom, which depends on the bough, which depends on the trunk, which depends on the roots, which depend on the soil, which in order to create new life depends on the seeds, which come from the apple. This is the cyclical view of creation which is ongoing, has no beginning, and no end.

If we superimpose the allegory of the apple upon the theory of Dependent Origination, we produce a fourfold formulation:

1 If the tree blossoms it will bear fruit.   So if *A* exists, *B* comes into being.
2 If the tree bears fruit, seed will return to the earth.   If this arises, that arises.
3 If there is no blossom, there can be no fruit.   If there is no *A*, there will be no *B*.
4 If the tree bears no fruit, seed will not fall to the earth.   If this stops, that stops.

There can be nothing that stands outside this cyclical concept of creation, since everything is entirely dependent for its existence on something else. To speak of a Creator God, existing outside and entirely independent of his creation, upon whom his creation is entirely dependent, is untenable in Buddhist logic. In Buddhist thought, there can be no such thing as divine birth, since this would negate the cycle of dependence.

Accordingly, we cannot speak of *dukkha*, nor of anything else for that matter, having a first cause. What the Buddha did identify, however, is an immediate (if not the only) cause of *dukkha*. The early texts are unequivocal that this cause is *tanha*:

> It is this "thirst" (craving, *tanha*) which produces re-existence and re-becoming *(ponobhavika)*, and which is bound up with passionate greed *(nandiragahagata)*, and which finds fresh delight now here and now there *(tatratatrabhinandini)*, namely, (1) thirst for sense pleasures *(kama-tanha)*, (2) thirst for existence and becoming *(bhava-tanha)* and (3) thirst for non-existence (self-annihilation, *vibhava-tanha)*.[11]

At the heart of the problem lies the false notion, caused by ignorance, that we have a permanent Self *(atman)*, and that this self has to be appeased, protected and prolonged. This introduces a craving, desire or thirst *(tanha)* to satisfy this so-called self. To this end, mankind embraces a whole gamut of ploys to satiate this thirst and thereby satisfy this supposed self. The folly is that the craving self-perpetuates not only the craving, but life itself, condemning mankind to continued rebirth on the *samsaric* cycle of aimless wandering. The greater the desire to satisfy becomes, the more mankind perpetuates the craving which is the palpable cause of suffering; this, according to the Great Physician, is the cause of all the ills of the world.

To dissociate oneself from the false concept of a self, on the other hand, has quite the opposite effect. Freedom from this belief, leads to freedom from rebirth and escape from the *samsaric* cycle. Thus for the *arahant*, the enlightened human being of Theravada Buddhism, liberation from *samsaric* bondage is assured. Since the *arahant* has no notion of an *atman* or permanent self, selfish desires are not present in his thoughts, nor do they manifest themselves in his actions. He certainly performs actions, but these actions are devoid of *tanha* and therefore do not produce *karma* (good or bad), which is responsible for rebirth.

Damien Keown makes the interesting observation that Buddhist sources often speak of desire in a positive light, thereby distinguishing between excessive or wrongly directed desire *(tanha)* and desire described in more positive terms *(chanda)*. On this view, not *all* desire is wrong:

> Whereas wrong desires restrict and fetter, right desires enhance and liberate. We might use smoking as an example to illustrate the difference. The desire of a chain-smoker for another cigarette is *tanha*, since its aim is nothing more than short-term gratification. Such a desire is compulsive, limiting and cyclic: it leads nowhere but to the next cigarette (and, as a side effect to ill health). The desire of a chain-smoker to give up smoking, on the other hand, would be a virtuous desire since it would break the cyclic pattern of a compulsive negative habit and enhance health and well-being.[12]

This is a nice point, because *any* form of desire (good or bad) will produce *karma*, and *karma* causes rebirth. This will need further examination when we look at the concept of *karma*.

The Third Noble Truth: the cessation of *Dukkha* – *Nirodha*

The Third Noble Truth affirms that release from *dukkha* is attainable by the elimination of *tanha*, the thirst or craving to satiate the supposed self. This extinction of craving *(Tanhakkhaya)* is known as *nirvana* (Pali *nibbana*). At this point the interested reader could well expect a description, or at very least an explanation, of *nirvana* to follow, and there is no shortage of such description and explanation to be found in those sections marked "Buddhism" in our libraries and bookshops.

Furthermore, if language is the high-watermark of our civilization, it would seem reasonable to expect finite definition(s) of what *nirvana* is to be within the compass of accomplished writers. Such definitions, though, have raised more problems than they have solved, for we are dealing here with Absolute Truth and Ultimate Reality, which are beyond language. We said earlier that if the Buddha's Enlightenment could be explained then it wouldn't be Enlightenment: the same could be said of *nirvana*. Our task is not to understand *nirvana* but to realize it.

The Fourth Noble Truth: the Path or the Way – *Magga*

Having gained experience of both the sensual and the ascetic ways of life, the Buddha concluded that neither was satisfactory. Accordingly, he set out to teach a path to *nirvana* which followed neither of these two extremes, but which was actually a middle path between them, more popularly known as the Middle Way or the Noble Eightfold Path. It should not be thought that the Buddha taught this Way "one fine day" nor that the path must be walked step by step in a linear fashion. Rather, the teaching that the Buddha gave over forty-five years advocated developing these attributes contemporaneously and simultaneously as far as one is able. To illustrate his *dharma* the Buddha drew a wheel on the ground, the wheel being a well-known symbol in Indian thought. To this wheel he added eight spokes, his point being that all eight spokes must function simultaneously in order for the wheel to operate smoothly. By the same token, the Buddhist cannot pick and choose those aspects of the Noble Eightfold Path which are appealing, but must try to practise them all at once.

In the Four Noble Truths the Great Physician drew attention to man's malaise, and in the Noble Eightfold path he prescribed the cure for this malaise. The prescription takes into account man's thoughts, as well as his actions and can be divided into three broad sections, which deal with Wisdom *panna* (Skt. *Prajna*), Ethical conduct *sila*, and Mental discipline *samadhi*.

Wisdom *(panna)*

1 Right understanding.
2 Right thought

Ethical conduct *(sila)*

3 Right speech.
4 Right action/morality and conduct.
5 Right livelihood.

Mental discipline *(samadhi)*

6 Right effort.
7 Right mindfulness.
8 Right concentration, or state of mind.

1 Right understanding: *Samma ditthi*

Central to right understanding are three basic doctrines of Buddhism – *dukkha*, *anatta* and *anicca*. The student of Buddhism will have studied the concept of *dukkha* as set out in the Four Noble Truths. *Anatta* (Skt. *anatman*) is the teaching that there is no such thing as a permanent, unchanging essence in sentient beings, in other words no self, soul, or spirit which lives on long after the mortal body has died. The Buddha taught that what is commonly supposed to be an individual "living being", or "soul", which gives warrant to the affirmation "I am . . .", is nothing more than a combination of the five *skandhas*.

The third doctrine basic to understanding things as they really are is the doctrine of *anicca*. This teaches that there is no such thing as permanence, for nothing ever is; rather, everything is in a state of becoming. As surely as the five aggregates which constitute what we call a person are constantly changing, so too is everything else. Lack of understanding perpetuates suffering as we strive to hold on to that which is impermanent – life and relationships being two notable examples. Right understanding, on the other hand, negates ignorance, one of twelve causal links which perpetuate the continuous cycle of death and rebirth known as *samsara*. With right understanding of things as they really are, the craving for attachment to people and possessions which causes so much misery becomes vacuous, and suffering is negated.

2 Right thought: *Samma sankappa*

> What we are today comes from our thoughts of yesterday, and our present thoughts build our life of tomorrow: our life is the creation of our mind. If a man speaks or acts with an impure mind, suffering follows him as the wheel of the cart follows the beast that draws the cart.
>
> Dhammapada 1.1 (trans. Juan Mascaro).

According to the *Dhammapada*, we as persons are the result of our thoughts; change these thoughts, and we change ourselves. So right thought or attitude implies that in your wisdom you want to be changed and cured. You must want to escape from believing that you are permanent, from the burden of *karma* and from the trials of craving, aversion, anger, covetousness and foolishness, all of which are *karmic* producing states of mind, all of which perpetuate the endless round of death and rebirth. Drawing an analogy between rebirth and the burning of a flame, the Buddha claimed that if a man is still aflame at death, with wrong attitudes and desires, the lamp will be re-lit in another life. Having dealt with wisdom, the next four steps along the path concern moral conduct.

3 Right speech: *Samma vaca*

Man's speech must be compatible with the Buddha's *dharma*, that is, he must speak the truth, his conversation must be edifying, and he must not engage in scandal or gossip. One should take care with one's words, not only for the sake of truth but to demonstrate control and discipline.

4 Right action: *Samma kammanta*

Right action is the expectation of correct moral behaviour. Since the word *karma* literally means "action" (not "action and reaction" as in commonly assumed in the West) our actions must be right in order to produce the right results and so end suffering. The Buddha was the first to make clear that it is the *intention* behind the action that is of ultimate significance, not unintentional action of an incoherent mind:

> It is choice or intention that I call karma – mental work –, for having chosen a man acts by body, speech and mind
>
> A III 415

Karma (karman) is frequently equated with the law of cause and effect that governs existence. As surely as the dropping of a pebble in a pond will cause ripples, so any action undertaken must have its effects. Causes and their appropriate effects are inextricably bound to each other. The law of *karma* states that whatever action a person undertakes in thought word or deed must create a consequence; negative actions will produce negative *karma* and positive thoughts words or deeds will produce positive *karma*. But when we throw a pebble in a pond, the pebble will cause the engulfing water to ripple immediately, while water some distance from he pebble will react later. Accordingly, *karmic* effects are not always immediate and the *karmic* charges produced will continue into the next existence.

The five moral precepts which every Buddhist should follow are outlined in the *Pancha Sila*.

5 Right livelihood: *Samma ajiva*

Right livelihood should be maintained in accordance with the *Pancha Sila* as well as being non-exploitive and generous in spirit. Any occupation which brings harm to others, such as the manufacture or sale of arms, tobacco, poisons, alcohol, gambling, or harm to other creatures such as butchery, hunting or vivisection are anathema to Buddhists, for these are the lifeblood of suffering.

6 Right effort: *Samma vayama*

We can only rely on our own individual effort to realize *nirvana*. This implies continuous hard effort and striving. For the Buddha, effort meant putting theory into practice, eliminating evil thoughts and cultivating good thoughts. In the *Dhammapada* the Buddha states that, "Little beautiful flowers full of colour but without scent are the well chosen words of the man who does not act accordingly." Right effort is the conscious will to overcome the undesirable and unwholesome states of mind to which we, being human, are prone, and to prevent the development of similar thoughts; to promote the development of good, wholesome thoughts and to maintain these.

7 Right mindfulness: *Samma sati*

Right mindfulness is a mindful awareness of four main areas of consideration, bodily activities *(kaya)*; feelings or sensations *(vedana)*; activities of the mind *(citta)*; and the arising and control of thoughts and ideas.

In connection with the body, special measures are required to rid ourselves of ignorance and enhance our mental development; concentration on breathing *(anapanasati)* being one of them. Concentration (yoga) leads eventually to enlightenment; there being stage by stage progressions which develop this. In connection with activities of the mind, we should be aware that our minds have a propensity to lean towards one or more of the three defilements – greed, hatred and delusion – and one should act accordingly to overcome this inclination. It has been well said that the only common factor *all* Buddhists have is the will to control the three defilements.

8 Right concentration (state of mind): *Samma samadhi*

In this state, the Buddhist is able to free the mind from all external thoughts and images that are disturbing or unwholesome. Right concentration refers specifically to the use of meditation as a vehicle to control and discipline the mind, to lose the sense of ego. The unfocused, indisciplined mind in its normal desultory state is quite unsuited to perceive Ultimate Truth, but meditation enables the Buddhist to do just this.

Meditation, therefore, helps the Buddhist to catch ever-increasing glimpses of the Truth, until *nirvana* is achieved. *Nirvana* means "blowing out": the blowing out of the fires of greed, hatred and delusion, and hence the end of suffering. The Buddha once said of *nirvana*:

> There is a sphere which is neither earth, nor water, nor fire, nor air, which is not the sphere of the infinity of space, nor the sphere of the infinity of consciousness, the sphere of nothingness, the sphere of perception, or non-perception, which is neither this world nor the other world, neither sun nor moon. I deny that it is coming or going, enduring, death, or birth. It is only the end of suffering.

The *Pancha Sila*

Central to the ethical principles of Buddhism is the *Sutta Pitaka*, the second of the *Tipitaka* (three baskets) in the Theravadin scriptures. The basic moral beliefs are shared by both schools. The *Sutta Pitaka* includes within its collection the *Pancha Sila* or five ethical precepts of Buddhism, and the *Dhammapada*, consisting of 423 verses of sayings of the Buddha. The *Pancha Sila* lays down specific rules of moral conduct that are really an enlargement on the fourth stage of the Noble Eightfold Path.

1 *To abstain from taking life*

This means abstaining from killing anything that lives. The crime is proportionate to the strength of the desire to kill. Five factors are involved here:

(i)   the presence of a living being, human or animal.
(ii) the realization or perception that it is a living being.
(iii) the intention to murder.
(iv) the action of murdering the living being.
(v)   the resulting death.

The individual who deliberately takes the life of a living being will reap dire consequences in the next life. Important, also, is whether life is taken at one's own hand or by instigation. So this first precept implies pacifism. Butchering, hunting and warfare are traditionally abhorrent to the Buddhist. This presents some moral predicaments for the practising Buddhist in contemporary life.

For some Buddhists today, it is debatable whether animals should be killed for food. This seems to be a question of interpretation as well as a matter of culture, many Japanese Buddhists being traditional fish eaters. Some Buddhists are strict vegetarians, others interpret the Buddha's teaching on this to suggest moderation, eating without indulgence. For the Buddha, however, one's relationship with all living things should be so close that to harm any living creature is tantamount to harming oneself. The Buddha taught that true sacrifice was not in the form of animals for worship or food, but of one's own selfish motives. The greatest sacrifice is made by the person who abstains from taking life and follows the remaining four precepts:

2   To abstain from taking what is not given

As surely as the first precept is wider than the edict "Thou shalt not kill",
so is the second precept wider than the law "Thou shalt not steal". Two
interesting qualifications are laid on this rule of conduct. The severity
of the sin depends on :

    (a)   the value of the property stolen
    (b)   the worth of the owner.

Traditionally, although a Theravadin monk is allowed to carry a
begging bowl, he must never ask nor beg for anything, but rely for sustenance on the generosity of the laity (who will offer him food only too
willingly in order to accrue good *karma*).

3   To abstain from sensuous misconduct

This is seen in terms of (i) mental misconduct, that is, the will to enter
into forbidden relationships, and (ii) physical misconduct in terms of the
physical action itself. Homosexuality is completely forbidden, and
taboos on females fall into two main categories :

    (a)   those who are within kinship relations who are also "claimed".
    (b)   those in a subservient position or "bought" women, e.g.
            servants, concubines, war-captives, etc.

4   To abstain from false speech

This covers all types of deception, even deceitful body language.
Hypocrisy seems an apt description here. To mislead someone willingly
or to misrepresent something is morally wrong. Here, again, different
degrees of moral transgression are noted. For example:

> If a householder, unwilling to give something, says that he has not got it,
> that is a small offence, but to represent something one has seen with one's
> own eyes as other than one has seen it, that is a serious offence.[13]

5   To abstain from intoxicants

This refers to alcohol and all drugs. The essence of this precept is that
one must have control over oneself, and one's mind must not be

clouded. Drugs and alcohol involve dependence on externally induced alteration of one's consciousness.

These then are the five precepts, and within them, abstention can take place at three levels.

(a)   at the intuitive level: we may feel that it is wrong to take life in a particular situation and actually refrain from doing so.
(b)   at the level of formal commitment to the principles, even at the expense of one's own life.
(c)   at the level of the saintly holy man who, on the Eightfold Path, has lost all inclinations and temptation to engage in practices which are not right.

The *Dhammapada* gives many other moral principles to be observed by Buddhists. Similar to the Christian ethic of "turning the other cheek" is the Buddhist teaching on forgiveness, "'He abused me, he struck me, he overcame me, he robbed me' – in those who harbour such thoughts hatred will never cease."

The Buddhist should avoid inflicting suffering:

That action only is "well-done" which brings no suffering in its train.

An additional three precepts soon followed the original five. These *Eight Precepts* were followed by early monks and the additions included what soon came to be regarded as a prohibition on eating after midday; abstaining from dancing, singing and revelry's attendant dress and cosmetics; and abstaining from using high seats or high beds, both normally associated with the wealthy. By dividing the *Eight Precepts* into nine and adding the prohibition not to accept gold or silver even when they are offered as gifts, *Ten Precepts* were formed. Many other rules were added and accepted by the monks of early Buddhism.

Sila, Samadhi, Panna

The Buddha's teachings fall into three broad categories – *sila, samadhi* and *panna.* The discourses have been given this authoritative grouping by compilers who have arranged the material in a manner which gives it a cumulative order. By way of illustration, we may consider the

Samannaphala discourse, found in the *sutta* of the same name, other-wise known as "The Fruits of the Life of a Recluse".

The discourse begins with an account of the rising up of an *arahant*. According to Theravada Buddhism, an *arahant* is a perfected being in whom ignorance, desire, wrong views and becoming have ceased. Derived possibly from *ari* "enemy", and *han* "to kill", an *arahant* is one who has "killed the enemy", the enemy being "desire". Alternative derivations include *arhati* "to be worthy of", which would render a meaning to *arahant* of "one who is worthy and deserving". An *ara-hant* has no sense of *I* or *mine*, but is dispassionate and totally free from attachment. *Arahants* were trained to achieve perfection in three areas – moral discipline, concentration and wisdom. In Pali, these are translated as *sila, samadhi* and *panna.* Having abandoned all that is foolish in word and deed, the *arahant*'s speech is considered to be a hidden treasure.

Sila

Time and again, Buddhist scriptures warn of the danger of approaching *samadhi* and *panna* without a thorough grounding in *sila*. The fact that the first of the three categories in the *Samannaphala* discourse is the section on moral discipline is quite intentional. However, it is to the *Dhammapada* that we must turn for the key to Buddhist ethics:

Mind precedes all things; all things have mind foremost, are mind made.

Indeed, this is the kernel of all Buddhist teaching, *for Buddhism is essentially a mind culture.* No person can advance (nor retard, for that matter) unless the seed for thought is first in the mind. Thus, the well-disciplined, indeed morally-disciplined, mind is a prerequisite for advancement to *samadhi* and *panna.* It is not only folly, but extremely dangerous, to attempt to progress to *samadhi* and *panna* without first attaining moral discipline.

By the same token, the attainment of moral discipline should be supported by cultivating *samadhi* and *panna,* for neither morality nor wisdom can exist in a vacuum.

Samadhi

Having enjoined the *bhikku* (novitiate) to the importance of *sila*, the *Samannaphala* discourse proceeds to a discussion of *samadhi. Samadhi,* the second important aspect of *arhat* training, refers to the calming of the mind, when one has withdrawn from sense stimuli. This Sanskrit word is normally translated "concentration", experienced in a trance-like state, but wherein one still has mindfulness and awareness. Evil thoughts and desires disappear, and one experiences an inner peace and harmony, a contentment with simplicity. The state of *samadhi* is often described as a flame which is totally still, quite unaffected by even the slightest breeze. *Samadhi* involves "guarding the doors of the senses". The *bhikkhu* cannot avoid *experiencing* sense stimuli, but he can avoid *reacting* to them. Once the mind can be guarded against such invasion, it can evolve. Within *samadhi* are three practices – *the eight dhyanas, the four unlimited,* and *occult power*.

1 The eight *dhyanas*

The eight *dyanas* are the stages by which one gradually transcends the field of sense perception, until one can "touch *nirvana* with one's body". Such proximity to *nirvana* does not mean that final salvation is now achieved, for the experience lasts only while practising the *dhyanas*. In later Buddhism, the Yogacarin school of thought concentrated particularly on this aspect of Buddhism.

The Buddhist term *nirvana* means "blowing out", and endless confusion has been caused by western writers who, in their misunderstanding, have interpreted this to mean the cessation of life. They conclude that, because of its emphasis on suffering, Buddhism seems to have a negative goal of extinction. *Nirvana*, so the argument goes, is the "blowing out" of the person or soul. How *nirvana* can have this meaning when the Buddha, in his second sermon, taught that beings have no soul, these writers never make clear. To suggest that a being with no soul can have the soul he never possessed "blown out", is linguistic nonsense. *Nirvana* does mean "blowing out", but it has nothing to do with the cessation of life: what must be blown out are the three roots of evil – greed, hatred and delusion. *Nirvana*, then, should not be seen as extinction, but as *extinguishing* the self-centred, self-assertive life. This is the destruction of the separate ego through which the world takes on its illusory form.

2 The *Brahmavihara*

In Theravada Buddhism, the *Brahmavihara* (otherwise known as the four unlimited), consist of four sublime states of mind: love, compassion, sympathetic joy, and serenity. The importance given to the

Brahmavihara is exemplified in the fact that this was one of the major aspects of Buddhism taken up by early Mahayanists.

Metta means "love" or 'active good will". *Metta* is the first of the *Brahmavihara,* and is a sublime state of consciousness in which loving-kindness is radiated to all humanity. This is an injunction to universal love. *Metta* is concerned with every quarter of the world, and all its inhabitants, to whom love should be given. Loving-kindness must become a quality of the thinker's mind.

So let a man cultivate love without measure towards the whole world . . . this state of mind is the best in the world.

The Discourse on Universal Love, *The Metta Sutta*

The Discourse contains the express wish for the happiness of all beings:

May all beings be happy and at their ease. May they be joyous and live in safety. All beings whether weak or strong – omitting none – in high, middle or low realms of existence, small or great, visible or invisible, near or far away, born or to be born – may all beings be happy and at their ease. Let none deceive another, or despise any being in any state; let none by anger or ill-will wish to harm another!

It is appropriate that *metta* should be the first of the *Brahmavihara,* for the Buddha taught by example that we should serve and love others. He is depicted as delaying his *nirvana* for the benefit of others and as caring for others by actively seeing to their needs.

As a result of *metta, karuna* is generated. This, the second of the *Brahmavihara,* is best translated "compassion", and is one of the two pillars of Mahayana Buddhism, the other being "wisdom". *Karuna* is the complete identification of oneself with the suffering of others, having total empathy with the sufferer.

Mudita, the third of the *Brahmavihara,* is the ideal of sharing joy and happiness. Besides one's own joy, this includes the ability to be joyful and happy because others are happy. One should share the joy of others even when one is not personally involved in the circumstances of that joy.

Upekkha is equanimity and serenity. The fourth of the

Brahmavihara suggests a balanced, calm approach to life when one is not swayed by excitement or one's own ego. What it most certainly is not is "indifference" – rather it is the ability to be active in the world without the involvement of the ego.

Panna

Sila, samadhi and *panna* are the three doctrines often used to epitomize Buddhism, but it is the last of these, *panna* (Pali) or "wisdom" (Skt. *prajna*), which is the keystone. While the *dhyanas,* the stages of trance, can take one to the door of *nirvana,* only with wisdom can enlightenment be realized. *Wisdom* pervades all *dharmas* and teachings of the Buddha. These, then, are some of the original teachings of Buddhism, many of which are fundamental to Zen in the twenty-first century, as we shall see presently.

4 Zen and the Mahayana Sutras

The roots of Zen . . . are to be found more immediately in the soil of the great Mahayana sutras . . . Another essential trait of Zen in its historical form is its total embeddedness in Buddhist religion. Zen sprouts from the Buddhist mother soil, and remains piously rooted in it. The great Zen masters are without exception spiritual men who are indebted for their best qualities to the Buddhist religion.[1]

Everything the Buddha taught was delivered orally; throughout his lifetime he wrote nothing. Indeed, a supposedly complete record of the Buddha's teachings was not committed to writing until some four centuries after his death. Nor did his uniquely precious legacy propose any consistent system of philosophy or metaphysics, for his thrust of thought centred upon the practicalities of spiritual liberation. Consequently, various schools of thought came into being. Within a century or so of the Buddha's demise, a group of monks calling themselves "the great *Sangha* party", the *Mahasanghika*, had left the mainstream *Sangha* to become what many scholars believe to be the seed of Mahayana Buddhism to which Zen belongs. The development of the two overlapping traditions, Hinayana and Mahayana, is seen by most modern scholars today to have been a gradual organic development, and not a radical split, as was earlier supposed.[2]

The most important literature for Mahayana Buddhism in general and Zen in particular is the *Prajnaparamita* literature. This began as a basic text formulated in the last century BCE and the first century CE, and was later expanded into a number of sutras. *Prajnaparamita* means

"Perfection of Wisdom", and is considered by the Mahayana to be the "second turning of the Dharma wheel", surpassed only by the fundamental teachings of Sakyamuni Buddha. The word *prajna* "wisdom" is an important one in Buddhism for it is one of the pillars of both the Theravada and Mahayana traditions. Mahayana Buddhism is based on the two pillars of *prajna* and *mahakaruna* (great compassion). Although in ordinary usage it can refer to intellectual analysis, *prajna* here refers to the kind of wisdom that is ultimate wisdom, knowledge of reality and the way things really are.

Because it is *ultimate* knowledge of the truth (rather than *conventional* truth), in this sense *prajna* is *perfect* wisdom. In Buddhism such wisdom, for most schools including Zen, is the key to *nirvana*. The *Prajnaparamita* literature, therefore, praises the highest and perfect wisdom that leads to *nirvana* while also setting out the perfections, the *paramitas*, of the path to the realization of *nirvana*. There are six of these: giving, morality, patience, vigour, concentration/meditation and, underpinning all, wisdom. These *paramitas* can only *be* perfect when they are accompanied by perfect wisdom. So the *Prajnaparamita Sutras* claim that perfect giving, morality and so on can only come about with the acquisition of ultimate wisdom, knowledge of the true state of things.

The problem is that the texts themselves are ambivalent and contradictory; in chapter twelve of the *Srimala-devi Simhanada Sutra* there is both a perfection of permanence and a Self, while the *Lankavatara Sutra* attests that there may appear to the ignorant mind a Self or an Eternal Creator, but this is really emptiness.

Although most scholars equate the wisdom of Mahayana Buddhism with knowledge of the total lack of plurality and dualities in all things and their commonality in emptiness, the fact that scholars are not of one mind over the *Prajnaparamita* literature highlights its complex nature, where contradiction is piled upon contradiction. We ourselves should be careful not to oversimplify the issues involved. Composed over many generations, the sutras are complex and far from clear, despite their ultimate goal of setting out a path to *nirvana*.

The *Lotus Sutra*, "The Lotus of the True Law", is one of the most influential in the whole of Mahayana literature. The great drama played out in the *Lotus Sutra* finds Sakyamuni Buddha as the cosmic Buddha in human form helping others on the same path to enlightenment that he himself treads. Great store is placed in the fact that the *Lotus Sutra* attests that all of the Buddha's previous teaching was provisional, since humankind could not have coped with being taught the highest truths in one fell swoop, and the *Lotus Sutra* crystallizes these highest teachings. The *dramatis personae* of the *Lotus Sutra* include buddhas and *bodhisattvas* as well as humans, and its message is unequivocal: Buddhahood is for all humanity, indeed, it is humankind's natural state. Chapter eight illustrates this point graphically in the parable of the priceless jewel. This has been sewn into a poor man's garment by a friend, while he is asleep. Unaware of his priceless gem, the poor man spends a year and a month fretting and slaving over this, that, and the other, while all the time he has everything he needs, but his ignorant, clouded mind won't let him see it. In similar fashion, we have lingering doubts that our own lives are really satisfactory, but because we are unable to identify precisely what is wrong, we act badly and blame others. With our minds in this clouded state of ignorance and confusion, we are quite unable to appreciate the immense beauty that surrounds us. This is a fundamental teaching of Zen.

The main *Prajnaparamita* text is the appropriately named *Mahaprajnaparamita Sutra*, "The Great Perfection of Wisdom", which contains much of the literature extant in shorter texts, the *Diamond* and *Heart Sutras*, to which Zen gives great importance, being cases in point. The last named is the shortest of all the *Prajnaparamita sutras*, a fact that lends itself well to the sutra's daily recitation in Zen temples. In this text, wisdom is related to the five *skandhas*, and the affirmation that everything is empty *(sunya)* of inherent existence is vocalized in Zen temples to the tune of *ku-ku-ku*.

On the basis of the *Prajnaparamita* literature (to which the Zen school regards itself as the rightful heir) as well as other sutras, two important schools of thought arose, *Madhyamaka* and *Yogacara*. In many ways, these two schools complement each other, the *Madhyamaka* concentrating on *prajna* and the *Yogacara* on *dhyana*, meditation. The famous four-line stanza purportedly spoken by Bodhidharma, however, has caused misunderstanding, and invited a like caricature to be drawn of the Zen monk. Posited *ad infinitum* in western literature as the fundamental self-definition of the Zen school, the first two lines attest that Zen is, "A special transmission outside the scriptures", having, "No dependence upon words and letters." All too often, this has been interpreted to mean that there is no place for doctrinal study in Zen training; indeed, as well as striving to dissociate meditation from Zen, Suzuki inferred that the sacred Buddhist scriptures were little more than trash:

Zen claims to be Buddhist, but all the Buddhist teachings as propounded in the sutras and the sastras are treated by Zen as mere waste paper whose utility consists of wiping off the dirt of intellect and nothing more.[3]

On this view, many western writers have adopted the position that, far from revering the sacred scriptures, Zen monks regard them as an odium, to be rejected accordingly. However, Robert E. Buswell Jr.'s definitive study of Zen Buddhism in modern Korea (where it is known as "Son") has shown this sentiment to be far removed from truth.[4] The monks there are well versed in classical Chinese (the literary language of Korean Buddhism), an understanding they have gained through doctrinal study in the monasteries. Most Korean monks do not even consider meditation training until they have acquired an extensive knowledge of Buddhist doctrine. In fact, Rudolf Otto made the point that the Buddhist scriptures "which 'must be burned' to come to knowledge" should be studied first; only then will Zen be properly understood. Nowhere does the importance given to doctrinal study acquire wider visibility than in the reading of Buddhist texts from traditions other than Zen, including the Pali canon. Pali texts were found to be particularly helpful to the Son monks in their efforts to overcome the inevitable impediments to meditation – lassitude, distraction and fantasizing – that their attendant Zen literature failed to address. Indeed, we will do well to remember that no school of Buddhism has produced more texts than Zen!

Suzuki presented Zen to the West as pure mysticism, beyond history and metaphysics and outside the remit of any religious framework, yet he refuted his own position by repeatedly stressing the close association between Zen and the *Prajnaparamita sutras* and the doctrine of *sunyata*. In fact, Chinese and Japanese Zen masters have echoed the basic metaphysical tenets of the Mahayana sutras throughout the ages. Similarly, Suzuki's assertion that, "the spirit of Zen abhors all forms of intellectualism",[5] has brought further confusion to the western understanding of Zen Buddhism, to the chagrin of modern scholars:

> I would like to clear up a common misunderstanding which is that the Zen tradition is in some way anti-intellectual, and that it disregards the sutras. The first patriarch Bodhidharma brought the *Lankavatara-sutra* (Consciousness Only Sutra) with him from India. In the Zen tradition, as in all Buddhist traditions, insights that arise from practice are always matched with the teachings of the Buddha or the Patriarchs. If there is a discrepancy, then that discrepancy has to be investigated a little more deeply. This is how study and practice are matched up, one against the other.[6]

It was Hui-neng, himself, who affirmed, "do not let yourself be bowled over by the sutra, you must instead bowl over the sutra yourself". Despite being illiterate, the sixth patriarch of Chinese Zen had developed such mastery of the sutras that he was able to expound them to anyone who cared to read to him.

The second half of the aforementioned stanza attributed by tradition to Bodhidharma attests that Zen Buddhism promotes, "Direct pointing to the mind; Seeing into one's nature and realizing buddhahood". Since it is self-evident that Zen is concerned with enlightenment, it would not seem unreasonable to suppose that its monasteries were founded in order that monks might achieve this aim through meditation. While it is certainly true that, for monks in the West, meditation is fundamental to Zen practice, we will do well to remember that not all monks enter monasteries for the same reasons, and not all Zen monasteries are in the West. The answer to the question, "Why do monks choose to enter monasteries?" is that there are probably as many reasons as there are monks.

> There are the careful detail men, who prefer to work alone on the monastery's financial ledgers. There are the gregarious socializers, who take charge of entertaining the lay visitors to the monastery. There are the dedicated contemplatives, who spend months isolated from their fellow monks, intent on their meditation. There are the dedicated scholars, who gladly spend an entire day tracing a single scriptural allusion. And there are the vigorous manual laborers, who are most content working alongside the hired hands tilling the fields or hauling logs down from the mountains.[7]

This is true of Zen monastic institutions in contemporary Korea, where, "the majority of its residents spend no time in meditation, and many have no intention of ever undertaking such training".[8] For the Son monastic community, a disciplined life takes precedence over one dedicated to meditation

Sunyata

The concept of "emptiness" as the true nature of all things is called *sunyata*, and it is this teaching which is the hallmark of the *Madhyamaka* school of thought; indeed, it is the main teaching of the *Prajnaparamita Sutras*. *Sunyata* is the absence of *svabhava*, own-being, in all things and is experienced through *prajna* (wisdom) as an ultimate truth of the universe. Nothing can have *svabhava*, for everything is dependent on other causes and conditions for its existence; nothing can exist of itself. When all life is understood from the point of view of *sunyata*, the emptiness of *svabhava* in all things, then it is senseless to grasp at anything in it and this factor concords with the second of the Four Noble Truths, that craving is the root cause of suffering in life. We behave as if things have permanent, inherent existence and try to grasp at them and keep them permanently, in order to be happy. Nagarjuna, within the Zen tradition considered to be the 14th patriarch of the Indian lineage, claimed that regarding *sunyata* as the true state of all existence is the very wisdom that needs to be acquired in order to cease such craving and grasping, and so realize *nirvana*.

So truth cannot be found in something that is, or something that is not, it can only be found in the middle point between these two dualities. Indeed, this is why Nagarjuna, generally considered to be second in importance only to the Buddha himself, made no assertions of his own and confined his philosophy to demolishing the arguments of others. By gaining knowledge of this middle point between dualities, finite definitions are transcended. The doctrine of *sunyata*, then, teaches the emptiness of all things in order to free the mind from its misconceptions about the finite world. This is the key teaching of *Madhyamaka* and a central concept of the *Prajnaparamita Sutras*. So important is the concept of *sunyata* to the *Madhyamaka* school of thought that the school was actually known as the *Sunyata-vada*. This emptiness, however, is neither nothingness nor a particular essence characteristic of all things; it is much more the idea that ultimate reality is something that cannot exist in finite things or in ideas, even the idea of emptiness itself. If, then, there is any ultimate truth, it is both inexpressible and inconceivable. It is debatable, however, if *sunyata* is even emptiness of emptiness, whether it could be regarded as a kind of metaphysical ultimate reality: scholars are divided on the issue.

Accordingly, there is no room for the proposition that Zen Buddhism can be studied within a vacuum, for the historical beginnings of Zen need to be considered from the point of Taoist and Yoga influence, the Buddhist sutras themselves, and the Zen masters who studied them.

Zen and Yoga

In fact, Suzuki went too far when he dissociated Zen from Yoga. For Suzuki, western audiences, even scholars, have the propensity to view the meditation movement of all Asia as a single phenomenon, with little or no difference amongst the multifarious schools. His objective was to stress the uniqueness of Zen; his consequence was to divorce Zen still further from its Indian roots. As surely as Zen is unquestionably a form of Buddhism, having its origins in the Mahayana, so does yogic influence unquestionably permeate subsequent Indian religious beliefs and philosophical systems, including Buddhism.

It is not without significance that experts writing on spirituality avoid defining the subject of their attention; responsible studies of Yoga do the same. No simple definition can embrace the rich and extensive divergence of this religious phenomenon, while at the same time capturing its essence. Patanjali's classical work on Yoga primarily uses a major textual source, the *Yoga Sutra*, which is generally dated to the second century CE, though earlier references to Yoga are to be found in Upanisadic literature. The origins of Yoga can be dated to prehistoric times, in the pre-Aryan cities of Mohenjo-daro and Harappa. The Indus Valley civilization is dated fairly consistently to about 2500–1800 or 1500 BCE, though an earlier date of 3000 or even 3300 BCE is not impossible. Excavations there have indicated that Yoga is likely to have been practised in this Bronze Age culture. Three seals appear to depict a figure that, in scholarly literature, is widely referred to as Proto-Siva, though this identification has recently been questioned. The seals seem to show

some kind of divine being who is seated identically on the three seals, with legs drawn up so that the knees are outspread and the heels are brought together. This is not, as so many writers like to claim, the identical posture of the great Hindu ascetic God, Shiva. Nor is it the traditional lotus posture of eastern culture, where the feet are drawn up on top of the opposite thigh. All that can be said of this seated figure on the seals is that the posture is a still one, a motionless one, and is a yogic one.[9]

The word Yoga derives from the Sanskrit root *yug*, and literally means "yoke".[10] Although the obvious inference to draw is that of our wayward and desultory minds being kept in harness, it is important to remember that the essence of Yoga emphasizes the unity of body and spirit. According to yogic philosophy, each individual is a microcosm of the cosmos. On this view, the basic yogic practices of bodily postures (*asana*), rhythmic breathing (*pranayama*), and concentration (*dharana*) are used to obtain final liberation by disciplining both the self and cosmic powers.

Although the Buddha would have been averse to the philosophical teachings of Yoga, he undoubtedly would have been familiar with the tradition. Parallels may be drawn between the various approaches to Yoga found within the Indian tradition and Zen Buddhist Yoga; these acquire visibility in the contemplative Yoga techniques touched on above, and include the seated body positions found in the practices of both traditions:

> the consciousness of a cosmic unity, the body–soul totality of the human person, the primacy of meditation, and the experience of liberation – no doubt represent its essential traits and can be found one and all in Zen Buddhism. In Zen they take a particular shape, but as with Yoga we remain in the context of Far Eastern spirituality. For Westerners, this commonality is particularly evident in externals, but this external commonality rightly points to an inner congruency as well. The Zen disciple seated in the lotus position, like the Buddha himself under the pippala tree, resembles a yogin. Like the yogins, practitioners of Zen strive to control their breathing and focus their concentration on one point, not of course in the same way in all the branches of Zen.[11]

However, important points of divergence between Yoga and Zen include the final goal itself as well as the methods employed to reach that goal.

5 Buddhism Reaches China

(Mahayana Buddhism) supplied metaphysical theses which first astonished and then enchanted the Chinese, not much indulged on this score by their own philosophers. The fundamental thesis of the Greater Vehicle, as it was spread in China, was that every man is right now in the condition of the perfectly accomplished Buddha, a condition which he has no need to attain since he had never left it; but he does not know this and through his ignorance he creates for himself the evil conditions of the sensible world, pure illusion which the knowledge of the Buddha dispels.[1]

I f we expect to find evidence of a seamless transmission of Indian Buddhism to mainland China, we will do well to remember that it is culture that shapes a religion and not the converse. In India, at the approach of a monk, every head would bow, but a Chinese emperor bows to no man, hence the monks had to concede this point and bow themselves. The Chinese had a strong work ethic, whilst the Vinaya Pitaka expressly forbade monks to work (out of deference to creatures of the soil), an edict that caused Confucians to label them "economic parasites". Clearly, such publicity would have won Buddhist monks few converts, and they were anxious to redress this accusation. Their changing attitudes are reflected in the fact that sixth century T''ien-tai (Jap. Tendai) monks are attested bringing in the harvest, while the eighth century Zen monk Pai-chang (Hyakujo) went so far as to state, "A day without work is a day without food".

The central notions that the missionaries brought to China from India and Central Asia had a twofold pedigree, being the principal tenets of Early (Hinayana) Buddhism, as well as Mahayana. Early Buddhism implanted into the Chinese mind the importance of meditative practice (with which it was already thoroughly familiar) and themes of practical morality but, as we saw at the opening of this chapter, the Mahayana had a far more difficult task. The Buddha condition may be realized through meditation, as the Dhyana school advocates, or by having complete faith in the Buddha's affirmation that all things are thus, as attested in the *Lotus of the Wonderful Law*, or by other means. Recognition and application of these teachings leads to the devotee's becoming Buddha, having saved all living creatures whilst in the Domains of Meditation of the Bodhisattvas. This was the message that the Chinese mind had to comprehend and accept.

The advent of Buddhism in China occurred during the first century of the common era, at the time of a flourishing Han dynasty (206 BCE–219 CE). Its appearance initially heralded the release from spiritual imprisonment of a Chinese people long (four centuries) suffocated by the confines of Confucianism. Although Buddhism provided a spiritually impoverished people with an enormous potential for creative energy, paradoxically, it also provided highly refined answers to questions that the Chinese had not raised; the problems for which Buddhism offered resolutions were not Chinese problems. The Indian mind was preoccupied with suffering, its cause and its cure, a concern that had never arisen in Chinese thought, since all deceased ancestors were venerated, regardless of karma. Chinese thought centred upon harmony with nature, while Indians sought to flee the world. In fact, the two doctrines were fundamentally at variance at almost every point:

> The Taoists sought the survival of the human personality; Buddhism denied the very existence of the personality: for the Buddhist there was no Me. Taoists claimed to make the body last indefinitely and to render it immortal; for the Buddhists the body, like all created things, is essentially impermanent, More than that, it has only a nominal existence – is a mere "designation", as they say – and the only things which have a real existence are the simple elements which make it up.[2]

Furthermore, the grammatical framework within which questions and answers were set was diametrically opposed to the linguistic structure of Chinese. The discursive, repetitive nature of Indian Buddhist literature, replete with abstraction, was at variance with Chinese literature, where familiar metaphors, directness and concrete imagery abounded. Equivalent concepts and distinctions were absent from Chinese thought, an absence that rendered their vocabulary bereft of the terminology necessary for meaningful translation of Buddhist texts and discourse.

> But Buddhism is rather a complicated religion for oral preaching; and the work of translation which alone could really make it known proved to be extremely difficult. In Han times the Chinese language, though it had been made pliant by an already considerable literature, could still express philosophical ideas only with difficulty. What was most troublesome was that, since the words were invariable, it was impossible to render precisely those abstract words in which the Buddhist vocabulary abounds, so translators had to put up with approximations. Even physically, moreover, the task of translation was carried out under irksome conditions. The missionary, even if he learned spoken Chinese, could not learn how to write it; he had to accept the aid of a team of natives who were meant to put his oral explanations into the correct written characters. A multitude of errors and blunders must necessarily have resulted.[3]

Some Indian monks were illiterate in Chinese, and correspondence with the Chinese scribe was only possible through an interpreter. "In these conditions control largely escaped the foreign translator, and it was possible for his Chinese assistants to introduce into their writings terms, ideas, interpretations, which perverted the meaning of the original text."[4] Indeed, meaningful translations of Buddhist documents and intelligible interpretations of Buddhism did not appear until long after the demise of the Han dynasty, when translators who knew both languages began working on the Sanskrit texts. It was not until the early fifth century that an Indian Buddhist, Kumarajiva (344–413), organized a translation bureau that produced works (both new translations as well as rewriting previous poor translations) that were immense in terms not only of quantity but quality also. Buddhism now began to rival Taoism in earnest and subsequent translation centres produced enormous volumes of literature until the early eighth century.

> Kumarajiva supported and further clarified the Mahayanist doctrine of shunyata. He brought Mahayanist ideas into the mainstream of Chinese thought, and paved the way for the development of the Ch'an School, the precursor of the Japanese Zen tradition.[5]

The spiritual climate of China provided the Mahayana with an opportunity to develop that was not offered on its Indian mother soil. Tolerance in the interpretation of its doctrines was the hallmark of the Mahayana, and educated Chinese of the early centuries began to regard Confucianism, Taoism and Buddhism as representing the religious mind of China. Indeed, as surely as the rise of the Mahayana in India saw Buddhism being reinterpreted by some as a school of Hinduism, so did its appearance in China, to which it brought a new doctrine of salvation, result in its identification with a barbarian variant of Taoism; the first Buddhist recruits were Taoists.

Despite having stricter discipline, and more profound doctrines bereft of alchemy, in the eyes of the Han Chinese the points of contact were so numerous that Buddhism was but another sect of Taoism. The absence of sacrifice in public ritual and the importance given to meditation in private practice, as well as respiratory exercises and fasting, were recognised as common ground. In its oldest translations, Buddhist technical vocabulary is widely acknowledged to be borrowed from Taoism; at his enlightenment, the Buddha is said to have obtained the *Tao*; the six bodhisattva *paramitas* (cardinal virtues) are described as *tao-te* or virtues of the *Tao*; the Chinese felt that Buddhism showed a new path to immortality, that Buddhist *nirvana* and Taoist salvation were identical and they called them by the common title, *wu-wei*, or "Non-Action", the precise state of the highest of the Taoist Immortals, and they likened the *arahant* to the Taoist *chen-jen* or pure man, a title found in the hierarchy of the Immortals. To the deep consternation of Buddhists, they found themselves being regarded as followers of an inferior variant of Taoism; devotees who had simply misunderstood their master. Nevertheless, it is true to say that early Buddhists in China benefited from this misunderstanding; perhaps it is not stretching things too far to say that Buddhism entered China under the cover of Taoism,[6] and the two religions developed alongside one another in the new China.

Bodhidharma

According to the testimony of Tao-yuan, in the standard Ch'an version *The Record of the Transmission of the Lamp*, one fine day sometime in the year 520 CE, a certain Bodhidharma left the aforementioned Indian mother soil, and travelled East.[7] Of Judaeo-Christian traditions, it has been well said that if there had been no historical figure called Moses it would have been necessary to invent him; the same may be said of Bodhidharma, for with no Bodhidharma there can be no understanding of the history of Zen. However, we will do well to remember that, pared of its legendary accretions, it is not the historicity of Bodhidharma that is called to question, but the lineage which is reputed to have directly transmitted the Buddha-mind. Indeed, Heinrich Dumoulin has asserted, "As far as I know, no Japanese historian of Zen has denied the historicity of Bodhidharma."[8] With this in mind, and considering the impact that the Bodhidharma tradition has had upon Zen, the patriarchate deserves our attention.

This Indian monk is credited with personally introducing Zen Buddhism to China, where it became known as Ch'an. Bodhidharma is acclaimed by the faithful as being the first patriarch of Zen in China, and the twenty-eighth Indian patriarch in direct succession to Siddhartha Gautama. However, the list of twenty-eight patriarchs who purportedly followed Sakyamuni, as if in some form of "apostolic succession", has no historical warrant; indeed, the entire Bodhidharma tradition is historically questionable. It is recognized today that, in their anxiety to prove a direct transmission of experience from Sakyamuni himself outside the sutras, later generations from the golden age of Chinese Zen, during the T'ang and Sung periods, fabricated certain sensational events and retrojected them into the life and times of Bodhidharma. The same generation may also have credited Bodhidharma with these famous words:

> A special transmission outside the scriptures;
> No dependence upon words and letters;
> Direct pointing to the mind;
> Seeing into one's nature and realizing Buddhahood.[9]

For faithful Zen Buddhists, however, these words epitomize the very essence of Zen, and the fact that tradition attributes them to Bodhidharma melds the quintessence of Zen with the personage of the Indian monk. Indeed, the "special transmission" of which Bodhidharma purportedly spoke encapsulates the heart of Zen Buddhist aspiration:

> This is the treasured heritage of Buddhism, the goal of the Buddha's quest: the insight born of enlightenment that he wished to share with all peoples. It is the fundamental conviction of those following the way of Zen that within Buddhism this special transmission has been especially entrusted to the Zen school.[10]

Indeed, for Zen Buddhism, the Zen patriarchate itself began with the first spiritual transmission. Tradition places Sakyamuni before a typical assembly of earthly and celestial beings, each waiting in silence, and in expectation also for the Buddha's words of wisdom. But the World-Honoured One respected and retained the silence, instead holding aloft a golden flower without comment. With the dawn of a smile on the face

Buddhism Reaches China

of Mahakasyapa, who alone understood the Buddha's action, came the dawn of the wordless transmission that continued from generation to generation until it was brought to sixth-century China by Bodhidharma:

> At that the Buddha proclaimed, "I have the Jewel of the Dharma-Eye and now hand it to Mahakasyapa". This transmission is said to have continued unbroken from "heart to heart", to this day. What did the Buddha show? What was transmitted? What is the Jewel? The Buddha raising the flower? Mahakasyapa's smile? Endless speculations will not reveal it – it is to be discovered each for him or herself, in the course of Zen training.[11]

Perhaps Mahakasyapa was still smiling when he handed down the Dharma to the Buddha's devoted disciple, Ananda, who consequently became the second in line of the twenty-eight Indian Zen patriarchs; these included such notables as Nagarjuna and Aryadeva, and ended with Bodhidharma. All schools of Buddhism are proud of their associations with Sakyamuni, and Zen is no exception. Indeed, the evident anxiety of Zen to trace the transmission of the Dharma directly back to Siddhartha, as well as the fact that Zen is so Chinese in style, are among the reasons why the historicity of the lineage has been called to question. This has long tempted certain scholars to focus their Zen studies not on the teachings of Indian sutras but Chinese masters: "Today we know quite clearly that Chinese Ch'an did not originate with an individual Indian teacher and that many of its roots lay deep in native China's thought."[12]

Like countless other religious figures of history, Bodhidharma has had his story embellished with rich and fanciful elaboration, his wondrous works exaggerated at times out of all proportion, and transformed to the level of the sensational. Nevertheless, the formation of these accounts, even as legends, served the dual purpose of emphasizing the validity of the wordless transmission of the Buddha-mind from generation to generation, as well as showing how a new method of meditation introduced by Bodhidharma could continue and perpetuate this transmission.

There are three credible historical texts, written by Yang Hsuan-chih, Tao-hsuan and T'an-lin, which bear reliable testimony to the historicity of Bodhidharma, none of which provides a biography of that worthy, of whom, frankly, we know little. All three texts affirm that Bodhidharma was indeed among those who travelled across China preaching the Dharma, advocating meditation, and visiting temples. In a typically abrupt and direct exchange with Emperor Wu (502–550), however, Bodhidharma is depicted condemning the worth of building temples and reciting sutras. This meeting (which is not attested in all our sources) presumably did little to endear him to this founder of the Liang dynasty, a practising Buddhist who was earnestly enquiring of Bodhidharma what merit his actions had accrued. Nor did Bodhidharma's later rejections of invitations to visit the northern court of Emperor Hsiao-ming win him acclaim. After crossing the Yangtze river, but before handing down the mind-seal to his successor, Huik'o, who became the second patriarch of Chinese Zen, Bodhidharma is alleged to have remained seated for nine years in meditation facing a wall, until his legs wasted away after ceasing to function. Another legend tells of the wrath of this wild-eyed, ferocious-looking, bearded figure, which manifested itself in his cutting off his eyelids, because he had fallen asleep in meditation; these fluttered to the ground only to arise as the first tea plant. Legend also has it that on no less than six occasions Bodhidharma thwarted attempts on his life by miraculous means, though our sources do not attest why anyone should wish to take his life. It is generally supposed that the patriarch met his demise in 532 at a ripe old age, though most of his life, his teaching, and his method of meditation remain, like the figure, shrouded in mystery.

A later account tells of an official named Sung Yun, who, returning to China from abroad, met Bodhidharma in Central Asia on the very day of Bodhidharma's death. In his hand the patriarch held one of his sandals; the other was found when they opened his grave.[13]

Hui-k'o

Equally arresting, even with the horrors of so-called twenty-first century civilization forever in our minds, is the account of how Hui-k'o (formerly Shen-kuang) became Bodhidharma's successor. Repeated entreaties to Bodhidharma, outside the monastery of Shao-lin-ssu in the freezing snow, were at first ignored and then acknowledged with the assertion that still more was expected of him. Suiting the action to the word, Hui-k'o produced a sharp knife, severed his left arm at the elbow, and presented it to Bodhidharma. Convinced at last of his sincerity, Bodhidharma now enquired of the agonized Hui-k'o what it was that he wanted:

"My mind has no peace as yet! I beg you, master, please pacify my mind!"
"Bring your mind here and I will pacify it for you," replied Bodhidharma.

"I have searched for my mind, and I cannot take hold of it," said the Second Patriarch. "Now your mind is pacified," said Bodhidharma.[14]

The instant realization which now dawned on Hui-k'o is known in Japanese as *satori*. The method employed here to induce the second patriarch's *satori* is said to be the first recorded instance of what was to become the characteristic *mondo* of Rinzai Zen. The *mondo*, or "question and answer" method of instruction, takes the form of a dialogue between master and pupil, engaged in with such rapidity that the sequence of logical thought patterns is transcended and intuitive knowledge is attained instantly.

Our information is scant on the period immediately following the demise of Bodhidharma, but if, with the transmission of the Dharma to Hui-k'o, there is the temptation to speak already of a "Zen school", then this is a temptation that must be avoided; clearly defined Zen schools did not materialize in China until the eighth century. The historian, Tao-hsuan, our main source for this period, tells that it was a middle-aged and well-educated Hui-k'o, well-versed in Taoism, Chinese classics, and Buddhist philosophy, who received the Buddha-mind from Bodhidharma; according to Tao-hsuan, Hui-k'o also received the transmission of the *Lankavatara Sutra (Descent to the Island of Lanka),* though the historical worth of this statement is, at best, doubtful. Evidently, Hui-k'o was the first to recognize the essence of the sutra, which focused on intuitive insight and self-enlightenment, though his efforts to disseminate this message were thwarted by the stance of those who supported the Wisdom sutras.

Even if it is premature to speak of a Zen school at this early stage, the Bodhidharma tradition was certainly a part of the growing meditational movement of the time, even though the acclaimed uniqueness of Bodhidharma's method and its subsequent development must remain concealed from us forever. Equally certainly, the *Lankavatara Sutra,* with its emphasis on intuitive insight and self-enlightenment, exerted a considerable influence on the meditational movement in general, and the Zen tradition in particular. Realization of this inner enlightenment, made possible by the Tathagata-womb which we all have, obviates recognition of any duality, since mental discriminations are now transcended:

The *Lankavatara* also teaches that words are not necessary for the communication of ideas. In some Buddha lands teachings are transmitted by gazing, moving of facial muscles, raising of eyebrows, frowning, smiling, and twinkling of eyes. Here one sees a definite affinity between the *Lankavatara* and later Ch'an practices. Moreover, the tradition of gradual enlightenment followed by Shen-hsiu and his adherents might also be traced to this sutra.[15]

According to one source, before his demise Hui-k'o handed on the transmission of the *Lankavatara Sutra* to Seng-ts'an (d. 606). Although the *Diamond Sutra* took pride of place over the *Lankavatara* in the southern Zen tradition, the northern tradition favoured the *Lankavatara*; such was its importance that we even read of the "Lankavatara School" in early histories of the Zen tradition in China.

The genealogy in currency in early eighth-century China concludes the patriarchate with Tao-hsin (580–561), Hung-jen (602–675), and the sixth patriarch Hui-neng (638–713). However, the historical reliability of the chronicles of the Northern and Southern schools of Chinese Zen upon which we have to depend for this information is at best questionable. All agree on the names of the first five patriarchs, though neither their order nor (master–pupil) relationship can be substantiated with any degree of certainty. In the arresting words of Fung Yu-lan:

> Such is the popular account of the early history of the Ch'an school. In actual fact, however, its development in India may safely be regarded as entirely imaginary, and even Bodhidharma, its alleged transmitter to China, looms uncertainly through the mists of tradition as a half legendary person.[16]

Hui-neng

What is certain, however, is that the attested dissent between the Northern and Southern schools over the authenticity of the sixth patriarch is an historical fact.[17] In 734 a southern monk, Shen-hui (670–762) suddenly challenged the position of Shen-hsiu, claiming that the fifth patriarch, Hung-jen, had handed on the patriarchal robe not to Shen-hsiu, but Hui-neng (638–713).

> He also attacked the doctrine of gradual enlightenment held by Shen-hsiu and put forward his own position in favor of complete instantaneous enlightenment, contending that pure wisdom is indivisible and undifferentiated, to be realized completely and instantly or not at all.[18]

While it is true that Zen masters teach sudden enlightenment, Shen-hui's conviction would find little support today among Zen monks in Korea, where they "routinely admit that they expect it will take upwards of twenty years of full-time practice to make substantive progress in their practice".[19] Sectarian controversy between the Southern and Northern Ch'an schools continued, with the Southern School, represented by the vociferous Shen-hui, becoming gradually the more powerful. Things came to a head when the Northern School charged Shen-hui with disturbing the peace, a charge that led to the banishment from the region of this now eighty year-old man, alienating public support from the Northern School, which soon fell from favour.

Nevertheless, it has been suggested that the aggressive behaviour of Shen-hui may account partly (but not entirely) for the fact that it was Hui-neng who came to be regarded as the symbol of the ideal that the Zen movement so ernestly sought. Although the final expression of Zen is found manifest in the *Sutra of the Sixth Patriarch*, the so-called *Platform Sutra* preached by the Sixth Patriarch Hui-neng, we will do well to remember that the new movement that gained visibility within Zen in eighth-century China was not the vision of a single creative personality, but the culmination of decades of complex evolution.

The standard Ch'an history of the eleventh century, *The Record of the Transmission of the Lamp*, has Hui-neng gaining the approval of the fifth patriarch over Shen-hsiu by a clever rewording of a stanza submitted by Shen-hsui to the patriarch in his quest for a spiritual successor. Hui-neng had already made an initial impression by asserting that everyone (not just northerners) possessed the Buddha-nature, an affirmation that was rewarded by his being appointed to the position of rice pounder.[20] The fifth patriarch, Hung-jen, was swift to recognize the genius of Hui-neng, but slow to announce his decision to monks whom he feared might become hostile to his selection. Instead, according to the standard Ch'an history, the patriarchal robe, the symbol of the transmission, was handed down in the secrecy of Hung-jen's room. Historians have been quick to point out that *The Record of the Transmission of the Lamp* was compiled some four centuries (and many legends) after these events purportedly took place, events that are unmentioned in the eighth-century work of Hsuan-tse.

An interesting anecdote marks the beginning of Hui-neng's mission as a Ch'an master. Evidently, he came across two monks in dispute over a pennant flapping in the breeze. The one argued that the only thing making the pennant flap was the wind, since the pennant was an inanimate object. The other contended that since it was only the wind that was moving, there could be no flapping pennant. Hui-neng intervened by asserting that there was indeed no flapping pennant, but neither was there a flapping wind; the only flapping was in their minds!

Until the third and fourth generation Hui-neng and his disciples represent the apogee of Chinese Zen. These enlightened masters burn Buddha images and sutras, laugh in the face of inquirers or suddenly shout at them, and indulge in a thousand absurdities. Though they may behave like fools and possess nothing, yet they feel themselves true kings in their free mastery of enlightenment. They know no fear, since they desire nothing and have nothing to lose.[21]

The Zen movement after Hui-neng

In Zen Buddhism today, the awakening of a Zen master is recognized and acknowledged or "sealed" by a process called "receiving the Dharma seal". This involves the master being given a transmission booklet by his teacher that traces the patriarchal lines back to Sakyamuni through the twenty-six Indian and six Chinese Patriarchs, and the various Zen lines in China, Korea or Japan. The demise of Hui-neng saw various transmission lines branching out, many of which are still extant.

Hui-neng's enlightenment coincided with the beginnings of the Tang Dynasty, and a now reunited China witnessed the dawn of the so-called Golden Age of Zen. The turn of the eighth century saw Chinese Buddhism begin to assume greater definition. Buddhism had long been seen as a religion in its own right, and had left Taoism far behind in popularity.

> Even at the time of its greatest development and imperial protection, Taoism remained far behind Buddhism in its influence; in Chang'an, the Tang capital, there were sixteen Taoist establishments in 722 as opposed to 91 Buddhist ones.[22]

Disciples of Hui-neng and his attendant teachings on sudden enlightenment were ubiquitous throughout China. These followers of the Sixth Patriarch held the conviction that the transmission of the Buddha mind could be traced back to Sakyamuni through Bodhidharma; the movement later became known as the "Zen of the Patriarchs" (Chin. *tsu-shih ch'an*; Jap. *Soshizen*).

> The dominant figures in the Zen movement after Hui-neng are Ma-tsu, Pai-chang, Huang-po Hsi-yun (d. 850), and Lin-chi I-hsuan (d. 866). Standing in a direct master–disciple relationship to each other, these four individuals help us focus the core of the "Zen of the Patriarchs": the trans-

mission of the Buddha mind outside the scriptures and sudden enlightenment through seeing into one's own nature and becoming a Buddha.[23]

The collected sayings (Jap. *goroku*) of these four masters were collated into a volume entitled *The Collection of Four Houses* (Chin. S*su-chia yu lu*; Jap. *Shike goroku*), that not only testified to the unity of the generation line, but to the advent of a "new Buddhism" in China. By the middle of the eighth century, these stories, discourses and sayings attest to the transformation of the legacy of India into what was unmistakably Chinese religion. The Indian Wisdom sutras, riven with paradox and dialectic remained, but the teachings now spoke of a reality in practical and tangible terms, using popular idioms familiar and meaningful to the masses, rather than that which could be realized only through abstract thought processes:

> What made Zen masters distinct was their use of common Chinese expression to bring Buddhism alive, through popular idioms that people could understand. Chinese poetry and folklore were used to illustrate Buddhist views. Taoism, being popular at the time, was often blended into expression, and conversely from Buddhist expression.[24]

There is a profusion of Taoist texts that attest to the fusion of Taoist and Buddhist ideas; just one illustration will suffice, allegedly penned by no less a dignitary than Chang San-feng, founder of the Chinese art of *T'ai Chi Ch'uan*:

> The rootless tree,
> Its flowers so red.
> Pick all the red flowers till the tree is empty.
> *Shunyata* is *samsara;*
> *Samsara* is *shunyata.*
> Know that the true *shunyata* is found in the midst of *samsara;*
> And when one fully understands the nature of *shunyata*, *samsara* disappears.
> The *dharma* lives forever, never falling into emptiness.
> This is called perfect enlightenment,
> And one deserves the title of great hero.
> The ninth patriarch achieves salvation
> And ascends to heaven.[25]

Where conflict did arise, Taoists sought comfort in the formulation of the incredible doctrine of *hua-hu*, wherein the Buddha was but an incarnation of Lao-tzu, who had gone to India to convert the barbarians before he became the Buddha. Accordingly, with both Buddhism and Taoism having a common source, there could be nothing improper in a foreign deity (Buddha) and the native deity (Huang-Lao) being worshipped by the common man at the same altar; clearly, the insistence of Early Indian Buddhists that Sakyamuni was a mere mortal was becoming ever less cogent. For the Chinese masses, therefore, a rather muddled theology arose that informed popular religion, a religion that borrowed freely from the teachings not only of Taoism and Buddhism, but Confucianism also, which had become the official religion by the time of the T'ang and Sung dynasties:

> we are reminded of the generalized folk saying that every Chinese person is a Confucian, a Taoist, and a Buddhist. He is a Confucian when everything is going well; he is a Taoist when things are falling apart; and he is a Buddhist as he approaches death. While this may have been intended to be taken cynically, it has been taken by some to indicate a kind of practical wisdom. This kind of practical wisdom is further illustrated in many folk temples in Hong Kong where one can see statues of Kongzi (Confucius), Laozi (Lao Tzu), and the Buddha set up alongside those of traditional Chinese immortals as objects of veneration.[26]

With the provinces of Kiangsi and Hunan lying "westward from the river" and "southward from the lake" at the centre of classical Zen, the powerful Rinzai (Chin. Lin-chi) sect emerged. Tung-shan arose as co-founder of the Ts'oa-tung (Soto) line, while Huai-jang was at the beginnings of the Rinzai line, though somewhat overshadowed by his disciple and successor, Ma-tsu, who boasted 120 enlightened successors. Tung-shan became enlightened upon seeing his reflection when crossing a stream. His realization is encompassed in his words:

> Avoid seeking him in someone else
> or you will be far apart from the self.
> Solitary now am I and independent'
> but I meet him everywhere.
> He now is surely me,
> but I am not he.
> Understanding it in this way,
> You will directly be one with thusness.

Sectarian divisions in Zen did not become consolidated until a thousand years later in Japan (Meiji period, 1868–1912), and Tung-shan's attention to detail in the five ranks (positions in practice) has consequently formed an integral part of koan practice in both the Soto and Rinzai schools. It was common at this time for Chinese to move between the teachings of masters of a variety of lines, or even become disciples of masters of two different lineages. An outstanding master of the time, Shih-t'ou (once a student of the Sixth Patriarch, Hui-neng), and his contemporary, Ma-tsu, would often exchange students. Shih-tou's famous verse, *The Identity of Relative and Absolute*, remains a standard chant in Zen monasteries worldwide to this day.

If the period from the death of Hui-neng (713) until the persecutions of Emperor Wu-tsung in 845 was the high-water mark of Chinese Zen, then Ma-tsu (709–788)) was the dominant figure during the third generation after Hui-neng.

> His appearance was remarkable. He strode along like a bull and glared about him like a tiger. If he stretched out his tongue, it reached up over his nose; on the soles of his feet were imprinted two circular marks.[27]

Unsurprisingly, given this description, violence was not outside Ma-tsu's remit; in the pursuit of enlightenment, he once forcibly twisted the nose of a distraught disciple to attain this end. Shouting *ho* (Jap. *katsu*) was another innovation he employed, a means to enlightenment later appropriated and promoted by the Rinzai sect. Indeed, the methodology became known as "stick and shout". Ma-tsu is the last Chinese Zen master to be given the title "Patriarch", appropriately teaching the dynamic Zen of the Sixth Patriarch. At the heart of Ma-tsu's message lay the unshakeable belief that since the mind is essentially pure, sitting in meditation in order to purify that which is already pure is folly. This is a lesson that he, himself, had been taught by his master:

> Ma-tsu was then residing in the monastery continuously absorbed in meditation. His master, aware of his outstanding ability for the Dharma, asked him, "For what purpose are you sitting in meditation?" Ma-tsu answered, "I wish to become a Buddha." Thereupon the master picked up a tile and started rubbing it on a stone. Ma-tsu asked, "What are you doing, Master?" "I am polishing this tile to make it a mirror," Huai-jang replied. "How can you make a mirror by rubbing a tile?" exclaimed Ma-tsu. "How can one become a Buddha by sitting in meditation?" countered the master.[28]

The so-called lamp-anthologies, huge collections of the teachings of hundreds of Zen masters, are replete with such anecdotes, some intriguing, some appearing to be diametrically opposed to the Buddhist precepts. The following account of Nansen Osho (748–834), one of Tung-shan's masters and a disciple of Ma-tsu, stands in direct contrast to the climax of the *Vimalakirti Sutra*, where Manjusri, the bodhisattva of compassion, asks Vimalakirti what it means to enter the Dharma of nonduality, and unreservedly applauds his "thunderous silence":

Nansen Osho saw monks of the Eastern and Western halls quarreling over a cat. He held up the cat and said, "If you can give an answer, you will save the cat. If not, I will kill it." No one could answer, and Nansen cut the cat in two. That evening Joshu returned, and Nansen told him of the incident. Joshu took off his sandal, placed it on his head, and walked out. "If you had been there, you would have saved the cat," Nansen remarked.[29]

The dictum from the *Rinzairoku* is equally well known, and equally paradoxical: "When you meet the Buddha, you kill him; when you meet the patriarchs, you kill them." Here, it must be clearly understood that the flowering of classical Chinese Zen witnessed not a development in devotion to Sakyamuni as the founding father of Buddhism, but a metaphysical transcending of all dualities. We will do well to remember that while knowledge is born of tuition, wisdom is the child of a single parent, intuition; in other words, your understanding must be your own, not something bestowed by the influence of someone else. This is the teaching here; anything that stands in the path of this transcendence must be summarily dealt with, and this includes any image of the Buddha.

A case from the *Mumonkan* makes the point. In hostile mood, a typical Zen master from the T'ang period, one Te-shan (780–865), (otherwise known as Tokusan), set out to vilify the notion that Buddhahood could be realized simply by seeing into one's own nature, thus rendering any study of the sutras redundant. Requesting lunch from an old woman on the way in order that he might "refresh the mind" Te-shan was asked what reading materials he had in his pack. On being told that Ts-shan carried commentaries on the *Diamond Sutra*, the old woman replied, "I hear it is said in that sutra, 'The past mind cannot be held, the present mind cannot be held, the future mind cannot be held.' Now I would like to ask you, what mind are you going to have refreshed?" A stunned and dumbfounded Te-shan later set fire to his commentaries.[30]

The blows delivered by Te-shan's staff, or rather the blows delivered by Te-shan's use of the staff, were part of his utilization of *upaya*, yet another example of the same "skill in means" employed by Sakyamuni, as a vehicle to enlightenment. "If you can speak, thirty blows! If you cannot speak, thirty blows!" he would shout at his disciples of the Rinzai sect. Another Zen master, Chu-chih, severed the finger of a disciple, who had the gall to emulate his master's custom of simply raising one finger in leading his disciples to enlightenment. As Chu-chih once again raised his finger before an agonized amputee, the disciple at once became enlightened.

Another of Ma-tsu's disciples, Pai-chang (749–814) is credited with promoting Ma-tsu's vigorous training, and formulating and applying monastic rules to his *sangha*. I have said before that it is culture that shapes a religion, which presumably is why one doesn't find too many naked ascetics in the polar regions.[31] Similarly, while "a robe and a bowl on a stone under a tree" sufficed the Indian mendicant, the dawn of Chinese Buddhism had seen Tao-hsin establishing a code of conduct for his five hundred disciples that necessarily demanded a day's work for a day's food; thus we subsequently find Hui-neng splicing wood and treading the rice mill for some eight months in order to gain sustenance.

Others followed suit, and though begging was not supplanted, additional activities included rice-planting, farming and bamboo-cutting. It was the monastic rules of Early Indian (Hinayana) Buddhism that informed Chinese Buddhism (including Zen), rather than those of the less formalized Mahayana, but Pai-chang borrowed from both, thereby establishing a new eclectic order. This new form of monasticism was thus independent of existing Buddhist orders and peculiar to Zen, its simplicity winning the approval even of Confucianists. Pai-chang certainly practised what he preached (alternating meditation and worship with manual labour), and in his advanced years he refused to eat when well-meaning disciples, who considered him too old to work, confiscated his tools. He produced two outstanding Zen masters in Kei-shan Ling-yu (Isan Reiyu, 771–853) and Huang-po His-yuan (Obaku Kiun d. 850); both became founders of Zen lines, albeit unwittingly.

Many western writers have taken the paradoxical contradictions that permeate the legion of aphorisms delivered by revered Zen masters at face value. This is because they have mistaken the lamp anthologies for historical documents that accurately reflect the circumstances of Zen monasticism. Accordingly, an image was presented to the West of a religious tradition that reviles all Buddhist scriptures, policed by a clergy that operates an intimidation policy; its devotees are subjected to mental anguish and physical abuse, supposedly in the cause of enlightenment, while anything that could possibly be considered to be of worth, *including Zen itself*, is steadfastly put to the torch.

> But such texts were never intended to serve as guides to religious practice or as records of daily practice; they were instead mythology and hagiography, which offered the student an idealized paradigm of the Zen spiritual experience. Many scholars of Zen have . . . presumed that they

provide an accurate account of how Zen monks of the premodern era pursued their religious vocations. They do not.[32]

It should be remembered that Zen is the language of poetry, and it should be read in this light: "What Indian Mahayana sutras state in abstract terms Zen does in concrete terms. Therefore, concrete individual images abound in Zen."[33]

The Five Houses

Thomas Cleary[34] reminds us that there is no "Zen Canon", carved in stone, from a body of holy writ whose teachings are to be memorized and recited piously. To look for the standard source book of genuine classical Zen is to look for something that doesn't exist, nor could it. Most Zen masters had no interest in history; they were more concerned with the needs of others than the deeds of themselves and taught accordingly. Zen masters were never idolized as in other religions. Consequently, Buddhist teachings came to be regarded as collections of useful ideas, devices with no necessary literal truth. In this light, strictly speaking, there can be no "History of Zen". Nevertheless, ninth and tenth century China saw the rise of several groups of outstanding Zen masters whose names became associated with the so-called Five Houses of Zen, and it is toward this direction that we must turn for the best examples of classical Zen Buddhism.

The year 845 saw China witness a persecution of Buddhism of unprecedented ferocity; by the end of the T'ang period, Zen alone flourished. The other outstanding figure in the third generation after Hui-neng was Shih-t'ou, and from these two great disciples developed what later became known in South Chinese Zen as "The Five Houses". Not to be mistaken for different sects or schools within the Zen tradition (though they later became identified as such), these so-called Houses were really lines of family traditions or styles originated by Ma-tsu and Shih-t'ou and followed and developed by devoted pupils. To the line of Ma-tsu belong the Houses of Kuei-yang and Lin-chi, whilst the Houses of Ts'ao-tung, Yun-men and Fa-yen are of the line Shih-t'ou.

Among these Houses are to be found what became the two major streams of Zen Buddhism today, Ts'ao-tung (Jap. Soto) and Lin-chi (Jap. Rinzai). The fact that the earliest of the Five Houses, Kuei-yang/Wei-yang, was short-lived, whilst the last to develop, Fa-yen, was probably the least significant, does not detract from the fact that their contrasting styles had much to offer. It has been well said, earlier in this book, that mysticism, like all other human experience, is influenced by human life conditions; it is not conceived in a vacuum. In this light, far from posing a threat to the cohesion and stability of the Zen movement after Hui-neng, the arising of the Five Houses, with their attendant differences in practice, provided the very foundation necessary for the development of Zen Buddhism in China. In order of historical emergence, the Five Houses are Kuei-yang, Lin-chi, Ts'ao-Tung, Yun-men and Fa-yen. Such is the importance of Soto and Rinzai that they each deserve detailed comment below,[35] but for the moment it is prudent to at least look at some of the distinguishing features of the Five Houses.

Kuei-yang/Wei-yang (Jap. Igyo) and the Circular Figures

Not without its critics, this earliest of the Five Houses made use of ninety-seven circular figures to symbolize enlightened consciousness and hence reality. Opponents were quick to point out that, far from symbolizing the true nature of reality, this *upaya* or skill-in-means device actually confused the issue since "the absolute emptiness and formlessness of all things" can hardly be represented by a number of different forms. Perhaps this is why the sect was short-lived. Nevertheless, outstanding personalities in the Kuei-yang tradition, such as Yang-shan, became enlightened precisely by this method, which they in turn introduced to their disciples. This rough and hearty sect saw Yang-shan amputate two of his fingers in order to convince his parents that he was serious about entering the monastery of Ta-wei.

Lin-chi (Jap. Rinzai) and shouting and beating

By the time of the Sung dynasty, the House of Lin-chi had become the most important of the Five Houses. Among the writings of the Zen schools, *The Collected Sayings of Lin-chi*, which records the founder's life and work, is held in high regard; it is Lin-chi of whom we have the most reliable historical evidence. Lin-chi, a highly gifted and intellectual master, achieved enlightenment only after being subjected by his master to a series of shoutings and beatings, and this, in turn, became his code of practice for leading his pupils to ultimate reality.

Ts'ao-tung (Jap. Soto) and the formula of the five ranks

Like the House of Lin-chi, the House of Ts'ao-tung remains today one of the two surviving Houses of Chinese Zen. The formula of the five ranks, though originating in this House, did not remain peculiar to it; both Chinese and Japanese Zen appropriated and employed it. This dialectical formula invites enquiry into the relationship between the Absolute and the relative, culminating in the final and fifth rank where there is total unity, often depicted by a black circle.

Yun-men (Jap. Ummon) and the "pass of a single word"

No less dramatic was the enlightenment of Yun-men, among the most famous figures of the later T'ang period. Evicted from the monastery by a forceful master who broke Yun-men's leg in the process, Yun-men became enlightened at that very moment. For his part, Yun-men treated his disciples with the same ferocity, often striking them with his staff and shouting *Kuan* at them when they were off-guard. Before he died in 949 Yun-men had gained the reputation of replying to profound spiritual questions with a single, apparently unrelated, word. Many examples are attested in Zen history; one will suffice:

> A monk asked Yun-men: "What is talk that goes beyond Buddhas and patriarchs?"
> Yun-men replied: "Cake!"

This type of innovative response became known in Zen as the "pass of a single word".

Fa-yen (Jap. Hogen) and the inner unity of the six marks of being

The last of the Five Houses was equally ephemeral, though far more gentle than the aforementioned two. Well-versed in both Chinese classics and Buddhist literature, its founder, Fa-yen (885–958) was a highly educated master, though his critics have questioned whether his erudition may have hampered his ability to teach in the true Zen spirit. His style, replete with sharp repartee and paradox, has been likened to the meeting of two arrow points, whereby the asking of a question is met head on, without explanation, by the repetition over and over again of an unrelated word or phrase. Totally steeped in the philosophy of Hua-yen (Jap. Kegon), Fa-yen was dedicated to the study of the *Avatamsaka Sutras*, particularly an understanding of the six marks of being, totality and differentiation, sameness-in-difference, becoming and disappearing, leading his disciples to a comprehension of their inner unity. The death of Fa-yen saw the demise of the House, and within a generation his Dharma successor, T'ien-t'ai Te-shao (891–971), had forsaken the teachings of his master and turned his attention to the science of the T'ien-t'ai (Jap. Tendai) school.

The Sung Period

The severe persecutions of Emperor Wu-tsung towards the end of the Tang period left Buddhism in general in a state of decline. By the middle of the succeeding Sung period (960–1279), but two of the original Five Houses of Zen survived, Lin-chi and Ts'ao-tung. Even the latter's future seemed insecure at that time, and it was to the Zen House of Lin-chi that Buddhism turned for survival. By the middle of the tenth century, Zen temples and monasteries of the House of Lin-chi alone were in profusion throughout Sung China. Though riven with political instability, the Sung period marks the high watermark of Chinese culture, with Neo-Confucian philosophy, Zen art and the Zen way to enlightenment among its lasting contributions. Not that Zen Buddhism was without its critics, and the Neo-Confucian movement that began in the Sung dynasty rejected Zen; indeed, Buddhists and Taoists alike were accused of turning their backs on Neo-Confucian ideals of humanity and righteousness.

These criticisms apart, the main threat to Zen was the temptation to fuse (or confuse) Zen with the teachings of other schools of Buddhism. This was made all the easier by the fact that an evergrowing Zen *sangha* still had neither doctrine nor systematized practice to preserve its uniqueness. To Zen's (at least, initial) chagrin, the school found itself being associated with the highly philosophical doctrine of T'ien-t'ai, as well as Amida (Pure Land) piety. Zen masters of the T'ang period had emphasized the superiority of enlightenment over study of the sutras and, under the fear of syncretism, it was not unknown in the Sung era for scriptural study to be condemned. The aforementioned *Avatamsaka Sutras* posed little threat since they were intimately allied to Zen thought, but other sutras were castigated. The mystical enlightenment of Zen and the piety of Amidism were coming to be regarded as similar experiences, while the rhythmic chanting of the name of the Buddha of

Pure Land (Chin. *nien-fo*; Jap. *nembutsu*), and the Zen application of *koan* practice were not seen to be too dissimilar.

It is the House of Lin-chi to whom we turn for the tradition of the koan. These "public notices" or "public announcements" (Jap. *koan*; Chin. *kung-an*) are 1700 in number and are found mainly in collections known as *The Gateless Gate* (Jap. *Mumonkan*) and *The Blue Cliff Record* (Jap. *Hekiganroku*).[36] It would be folly to assume that Lin-chi had a monopoly on koan compilation, however, and from the House of Ts'ao-tung comes a collection of 100 Zen dialogues known as the *Book of Serenity*.[37] Indeed, at the time, koan study was not the sole preserve of Rinzai Zen, as is often thought, for students in the Soto line were also guided by this means. It was not until Zen Buddhism reached Japan, and sectarianism later became an issue that koan study declined in the house of Ts'ao-tung, and *shikantaza* remained its main practice. *Shikantaza* has best been described as "quiet sitting in open awareness, reflecting directly the reality of life". This was and is the primary practice of the Soto Zen school. Soto and Rinzai were openly critical of the methods employed by the other, yet neither questioned the other's achievements.

So Indian Buddhist teaching was introduced to the Chinese mind. Its assimilation lost nothing of the Chinese feeling for life, yet melded Indian metaphysics with Taoist thought. Nor must we lose sight of the fact that the Zen masters never deviate from the frame of reference of Buddhist teaching. At no point does talk of destroying the Buddha, his Patriarchs, or his images (even when the last named *are* burned!) represent the reviling of Sakyamuni Buddha. These are symbolic gestures that emphasize that understanding is born of self-revelation, not the imparted teaching of another by means of the spoken or written word. "Once the intoxication of enthusiasm is over, the Zen monks assemble before the Buddha image for the ritualistic reading of the sutras."[38] The legacy of China to Zen Buddhism is considerable. It was here that Zen was given and maintained a maturity that it enjoys today; it was here that Zen blossomed and developed the ability to retain its essence while ever adapting to new cultures worldwide.

6 The Transition from China to Japan

The Japanese masters contributed nothing substantial to the teachings and methods of Zen. The Transition from China to Japan
Heinrich Dumoulin

The cultural influence of Rinzai Zen

It was from China that Japanese culture gained some of its now
famous cultural and aesthetic artistic characteristics as in archi-
tecture, gardening, water-colour painting, literature and
ceramics. The martial arts from China were attractive to the
Samurai warriors of Japan, so much so that Rinzai Zen became
the faith of the warrior. This was because it taught that the warrior could
engage in warfare and still participate in the spiritual life because the two
were, in reality, one. The martial arts of judo, *kung fu*, *karate*, archery
and fencing were engaged in from the Taoist point of view of *wu-wei*,
action rooted in inaction, and from the point of intuitive knowledge, not
simply the mastery of skills. In archery, for example there was no aim
to hit the target, but to bring the deeper intuitive knowledge into the
action, to let the self disappear, and to "go with" the action.[1] The
Confucian orderliness and properness may be seen behind the famous
Tea Ceremony, which is a religious and ritualistic ceremony used at
group meditations. Here, everything is prepared and carried out with
the utmost concentration, silence, gracefulness and serenity, an act of
meditation just to watch.

One of the most beautiful expressions of Rinzai Zen is its Haiku
poetry. Haiku poems, confined to a mere seventeen syllables, express

the affinity of humankind with nature and have something of the Taoist touch about them in their utter simplicity and yet paradoxical depth. They express quietness and spontaneity, suchness of things and an element of mystery. Some examples follow:

In the dark forest
A berry drops
The sound of water[2]

The thief
Left it behind
The moon at the window[3]

A fallen flower
Returning to the branch?
It was a butterfly[4]

The great Japanese Master, Basho (1644–94), composed the following:[5]

Spring rain –
under trees
a crystal stream.

If I'd the knack
I'd sing like
cherry flakes falling.

Wake, butterfly –
it's late, we've miles
to go together.

Come, see real
flowers
of this painful world.

Spider, are you
Crying – or
the autumn wind?

The earliest period of recorded Japanese history attests to the initial appearance of Buddhism in that country; an image of Buddha (Jap. *Hotoke*) arrived from Korea shortly afterwards in the year 552. Initial opposition to this new religion was soon overcome, and by the time of prince-regent Shotoku Taishi (572–621), the primitive *kami* cults of Shinto had become dominated by Buddhism. The prince-regent devoutly promoted Buddhism, and found the spirit and doctrine of the Mahayana to be crystallized in the *Vimalikirti Sutra*, otherwise known as "The Way of Enlightenment for All". The sutra itself, which emphasizes right meditation, and particularly the prince-regent's devotion to it, later exerted a considerable influence on the history of Zen.

In fact, the ancient chronicles of Japan attest to the appearance of Zen in that country as early as 654, when the eminent Japanese Buddhist monk, Dosho, returned from China and demonstrated his conviction in Zen by constructing the first Zen hall in Japan. Chinese Zen masters soon returned the compliment and their visits to Japan were not without a following. Nevertheless, Zen was but one of several schools of Buddhism in Japan at the time, by no means the most popular; meditation was forced to play second fiddle to the philosophical speculation and magical extravagance of Tendai and Shingon. Buddhism in general had fallen into decay and remained so for three centuries; by the end of the Heian period (794–1192) a decadent court had polluted not only the populace, but the Buddhist monasteries themselves.

By the middle of the twelfth century, Japanese Buddhism had all but lost touch with its people. The old schools of Tendai and Shingon, together with Hosso and Kegon, had become totally power conscious, with incomprehensible (to the laity) magical rites seen by the monks as being far more important than any quest for enlightenment. As the days, as well as the charisma, of Sakyamuni Buddha began to distance themselves in time from the memory of Buddhist minds, the path to enlightenment became increasingly difficult, and certain texts espoused a declining view of history, where *Mappo* marked the third and most degenerate stage of the Buddha's *dharma*, when no individual could attain enlightenment in a single lifetime. Appropriately named "The Latter Days of the Law", all that remained of the Buddha's memory were his teachings; practices were a thing of the past and "enlightenment" a mere word.

From the Kamakura period (1185–1333) came a cry for help, "a cry from a burning house", to use the imagery of the *Lotus Sutra*. Clearly, the time was ripe for a Buddhist revival, and the cry was answered not only by Zen masters, but by towering personalities from what became the schools of Nichiren and Pure Land. Onto the stage of twelfth-century Japan's history also strode Myoan Eisai.

Myoan Eisai (1141–1215)

Generally regarded as the founder of Japanese Zen Buddhism, perhaps it would be more correct to say, "Eisai . . . later came to be considered the founder of Zen in Japan."[6] This reservation needs to be applied since, though he undoubtedly stood at the beginning of an important development, it cannot be maintained that his efforts to establish a Japanese Rinzai school were successful. This was due in no small part to the resistance of the powerful Tendai monks.

Ironically, it was Tendai Buddhism to which Eisai was originally affiliated, becoming a monk in his youth; even when he later introduced Zen to Japan, both Tendai and Shingon influence were conspicuous in his teaching. Hopeful of securing a revival of Buddhism in Japan, Esai was impressed, though not consumed, by the Ch'an Buddhism he had encountered on his first visit to China in 1168. Ever mindful of the need to return to its roots, Esai then determined to examine Buddhist sources on the Indian mother soil, but his plans were thwarted on his second visit to China (1187–1191). He was left with no alternative but to reconsider the Ch'an Buddhism he had encountered in China earlier.

Entering a Ch'an monastery, Esai devoted himself to the study of *tso-ch'an* (Jap. *zazen*) and *kung-an* (Jap. *koan*). His efforts were acknowledged by his being presented with the Dharma Seal (*Inka*) of succession in the Huang-lung (Jap. *Oryo*) line of transmission. In his capacity as dharma heir of the Lin-chi school, Esai introduced this into Japan. His affinities to Tendai and Shingon were well known and Esai was able to build the first Rinzai temple in Japan, Shofukuji, unopposed. When, in 1194, he later proclaimed the superiority of Zen over other Buddhist schools, however, his Tendai opponents succeeded in raising a prohibition, and Esai was forced to make concessions, introducing practices other than Zen into the Rinzai temple at Hakata. Conscious of the fact that the time was not ripe for the establishment of an independent Zen school in Japan, Esai conceded a place in Zen to both Shingon (whose sutras he recited until his death) and Tendai.

Enni Ben'en (1201–1280)

Even after the death of Esai, the older schools of Japanese Buddhism still made their presence felt in Zen, and the Kamakura period of this time again failed to witness the dawn of an independent Zen school in Japan. Nevertheless, the considerable efforts of Enni Ben'en, better known (posthumously) as Shoichi Kokushi, certainly widened the acceptance of Zen in Japan and, equally certainly, increased an interest in meditation that had waned with the demise of Esai. Like Esai, Enni was not averse to including received rites from older Japanese Buddhism into Zen practice, and it was to the Chinese Zen masters in Japan, during the second half of the Kamakura period, that we have to look for an unadulterated Ch'an teaching, bereft of received rites from the older Japanese Buddhist schools.

Dogen Kigen (1200–1253)

The figure that towers above all others in Japan's religious history is Zen master Dogen. Acknowledged as having an incomparable depth of thinking, it may not be overstating the case to describe Dogen as *the* most influential figure in Japanese religious thought. His overwhelming desire to bring to fruition the reform of Japanese Buddhism saw this worthy introduce Soto Zen to Japan upon his return from China (1223–1227). A measure of the esteem in which he is held today is depicted by the fact that it is not only Soto Zen Buddhists who venerate him; he is still admired throughout the Buddhist World for his penetrating insight and depth of thought.

The transitory nature of all life was forcibly brought home to Dogen with the loss of both parents before his eighth year. Determined to attain enlightenment, he decided to renounce the world, and at the age of thirteen Dogen was ordained a Tendai monk. His enquiring mind was tormented by a question to which no one could give a satisfactory answer, "If all sentient beings are the Buddha-nature, then why is it necessary to engage in ascetic practices to realize it, and why do all Buddhas and Bodhisattvas aspire to raise the *Bodhicitta*, the Way-seeking mind?" Tormented by this question, Dogen left his solitary cell, deep in the mountains, and forsook the metaphysical teachings of Tendai. When he turned to the simple faith of Pure Land, his sincerity was recognized and he was directed to Esai. Frequently presented in Buddhist literature as a disciple of Esai, there is no written record of the two actually having met. Be this as it may, Dogen certainly entered the Kenninji temple, becoming a pupil of Myozen, Esai's successor. The eclectic nature of the Kenninji temple saw Dogen exposed to the teachings of Tendai, Shingon and Zen, though the last-named alone was new and intriguing to him. He warmed both to Myozen and to the strict stick and shout methods of the Rinzai school, though he still felt unfulfilled spiritually. Accordingly, the spring of 1223 saw both pupil and master leave Kenninji and set sail for China.

Arriving in port in central China, Dogen was given a profound example of Zen Buddhism in action. Encountering a Zen monk in the city stocking up with provisions, Dogen invited him back to the ship. The monk declined the invitation on the grounds that it was far more important for him to return to his kitchen service in the monastery. In Zen, daily service to the community is not only selfless, but a religious practice too, a manifestation of enlightened behaviour. Dogen's exposition, *Instruction for the Tenzo (Head Cook)*, is still followed in Japanese temples today. Its observance, together with sitting meditation and reading of the sutras, can lead to enlightenment. The seal of enlightenment was denied Dogen at first, despite his wandering from temple to temple and studying under the noted abbots of Tien-t'ung-szu monastery, Wu-chi and, later, Ju-ching (1163–1268). The harsh discipline of the latter, with his interminable periods of meditation, punctuated only by his stick and shout tactics, was ideally suited to Dogen, and at long last he received the seal of enlightenment from Ju-ching.

His mantle was that of the Soto Zen sect, though upon his return to Japan, Dogen had no wish to found yet another school, which, like the rejection of the sutras, he considered injurious to Buddhism. Instead, he embarked upon writing his first treatise on *zazen*, sitting meditation, entitled *Fukanzazengi*, for this is where his focus was. The degenerate climate of the age of *Mappo* had fostered a decline in moral standards at the Kenninji temple, and Dogen repaired to a small rural temple near Fukakusa. It was here that Dogen began his monumental *zazen* work, *Shobogenzo*. His ardent zeal for sitting meditation was unsurpassed, for this is where he saw realization of the true Dharma. In 1236, this belief culminated in the establishment of Japan's first totally independent Zen temple, at Koshohorinji. Shortly after completing the final chapter of *Shobogenzo*, Dogen entered mortality on August 28, 1253.

Zen after Dogen

It is ironic that Dogen had no wish to introduce a new form of Buddhism to Japan, for this is exactly how the people saw it. Indeed, Soto became the most popular school of Zen in Japan. The people saw Soto as being close to their hearts and close to the soil, so much so that a saying arose, "Rinzai for the shogun; Soto for the peasants." The demise of Dogen saw political turmoil in Japan, so it comes as no surprise to learn that Rinzai's appeal to the (warrior classes) *Samurai* forced Soto to take second place. Dogen came to be far from people's minds, even in his own school, and it was not until the nineteenth century that he became popular again.

It was during the days of Zen master Ikkyu Sojun (1394–1481) that Haiku writing, archery and the Tea ceremony became popular. Like Dogen, Ikkyu emphasized the transitory nature of life. Ikkyu also recognized the degeneration of Zen, and his poetry reflected the decadent times of the fifteenth and sixteenth centuries, when religiosity came to prominence at the expense of enlightenment. Symbolic imagery in the form of *mandalas* began to be emphasized, and Shingon Buddhism began to influence Zen in as much as Zen study became a secret oral transmission, much to the iconoclastic Ikkyu's chagrin:

Who among Rinzai's descendants really transmits his Zen?
It is concealed in this Blind Donkey.
Straw sandals, a bamboo staff, an unfettered life –
You can have your fancy chairs,
Meditation platforms, and fame-and-fortune Zen.

Two hundred years of civil war were brought to an end at the terminus of Japan's middle ages. Tokugawa Ieyasu (1542–1616) founded the third and final shogunate, and Edo (modern Tokyo) became the new capital. This heralded a rejuvenation of the people and a revitalization of Zen Buddhism. People now recognized the folly of relying on a so-called secret oral transmission, and Zen master Bankei (1622–93) urged them to abandon the koan and ancient teachings, and simply "listen to the unborn Buddha-heart". Bankei spoke the language of the people, and his popularity is unsurpassed; it is said that he had the ear of fifty thousand followers. For Bankei, overcoming the passions by absorbing oneself in the task in hand is the nearest we need to get to any secret transmission. It is the passions, however, that overcome us, concealing the very Buddha-heart that we all should heed.

An impulsive farm worker, admitting his nature, once asked Bankei for advice. The master replied:

Since all men possess the unborn Buddha-heart from their birth, you are now seeking for the first time to follow it. If you perform your chores with all your might, you are practicing the unborn heart. Also if while hoeing in the field you speak with the people and hoe at the same time, then you hoe while speaking and you speak while hoeing. But if you hoe in anger, your anger is an evil work which deserves the punishment of hell, and your work is toilsome and painful. But if you hoe without the clouds of anger or other passions, your work will be easy and pleasant. This comes from the Buddha-heart and is unborn and eternal labor.[7]

Heinrich Dumoulin reminds us that, "The Japanese masters contributed nothing substantial to the teachings and methods of Zen, and yet . . . no other Japanese master expressed the traits peculiar to his people as purely as did Hakuin, who for this reason is highly esteemed by all Zen adherents."[8] Indeed, it is not overstating the case to say that the form of Buddhism that gains visibility today as Rinzai Zen is a direct result of the revitalized reforms of Hakuin Ekaku (1689–1769); this includes one-to-one interviews between master and pupil *(dokusan)*, intensive meditation retreats, and dharma talks. All lineages of the Rinzai masters in Japan today come down from Hakuin.[9]

Like Bankei, Hakuin spoke the language of the people, and he undertook extensive social work among the poor. He was never an accomplished artist, though he amused everyone with some of his Buddhist caricatures. More importantly, he strove to give meaning to Buddhist practices and teachings that were previously taught only in a strict monastic setting. This is not to suggest that Hakuin diminished the importance of a well-regulated monastic atmosphere; far from it. For Hakuin, *zazen* lay at the heart of Zen practice, punctuated by honest, selfless work. His definitive work, *Hakuin Zenji's Praise of Zazen*, can be heard chanted in Japan to this day.[10] He wrote:

> For penetrating to the depths of one's own true self-nature and for attaining a vitality valid on all occasions, nothing can surpass meditation in the midst of activity.[11]

Following an intensely emotional enlightenment experience, Hakuin undertook to train his students according to the strict methods inherited from Tang and Sung China. Disparate strands of Rinzai training were systematized, and a koan study introduced that was graduated according to difficulty. Beginning with what is nowadays called the First Koan, Joshu's *Mu*, the student would be led, by means of intensive study, through a series of koans. "What is the sound of one hand clapping?" is another well-known koan attributed to Hakuin.

In the Soto school, enlightenment itself *(satori)* and koan study fell in and out of favour, with seventeenth-century reformers re-assessing the value of both. The Meiji Restoration (1868–1912) meanwhile, saw the establishment of Shinto as the state religion. Based on the divinity of the emperor, Shintoism began to usurp Buddhism, with many Buddhist temples being converted into Shinto shrines and Buddhist monks themselves becoming secularized by the new government. All forms of monastic Buddhism fell from grace, and reformers such as Nantembo (1839–1925) concentrated his efforts on leading Zen retreats outside monastic training. In recent times, a new lineage emerged that combined the teachings of both Soto and Rinzai Zen.

Shaku Soen (1856–1919) extended the horizons of Buddhism, both in terms of his broad compass and his unique ability to explain Buddhism in rational and scientific terms. Speaking in 1893 at the World Parliament of Religions in Chicago, Soen introduced Buddhism to the West as a practical religion rather than mere academic study as it had been previously regarded. And, as we have seen, Soen's student was Suzuki Daisetz Teitaro.

Part II
Zen Practice

The Ten Oxherding Pictures clearly illustrate the need for consistent dedication to practice after awakening. Although the kensho stories spotlight the third picture in particular – the stage of seeing the Ox – the fourth through tenth pictures map the higher stages of spiritual development to be realized through continued practice.[1]

7 Meditation

Sitting astride the senses is a shadowy, phantom-like figure with insatiable desires and a lust for dominance. His name? Ego, Ego the Magician, and the deadly tricks he carries up his sleeve are delusive thinking, greed and anger. Where he came from no one knows, but he has surely been around as long as the human mind. This wily and slippery conjurer deludes us into believing that we can only enjoy the delights of the senses by delivering ourselves into his hands.[2]

Since the words "Zen" and "meditation" are often used synonymously, it is fitting that we open Part II of this book by examining their relationship more closely. In his Introduction to *Zen Buddhism: A History*, Heinrich Dumoulin states:

Zen (Chin., Ch'an, an abbreviation of *ch'an-na*, which transliterates the Sanskrit term *dhyana* or its Pali cognate *jhana*, terms meaning "meditation") is the name of a Mahayana Buddhist school of meditation originating in China and characterized by the practice of meditation in the lotus position (Jpn., *zazen*; Chin., *tso-ch'an*) and the use of the koan (Chin., kung-an), as well as by the enlightenment experience of *satori*.[3]

It is true that Zen is normally translated "meditation", and Zen practice is certainly characterized by sitting meditation, but in the course of its development in China it became clear that meditation is the means and not the end – the aim of Zen is to realize *prajna* (intuitive knowledge and power): "The power grows out of Dhyana, but Dhyana in itself does not constitute Prajna, and what Zen aims to realize is Prajna and not

Dhyana."⁴ Undoubtedly, the practice of sitting meditation or *dhyana* was universal among Buddhist monks at this time, but with no necessary affiliations to either a *dhyana* school or a Zen school in India, China, or anywhere else for that matter. Indeed, the presence of a *dhyana* school is unattested in Indian Buddhist literature:

> the special instructors who supervised this practice were called *dhyana* masters, no matter what their school or sect. There were likewise *vinaya* masters, or instructors in monastic discipline, and *dharma* masters, or instructors in doctrine. Zen became a distinct school only as it promulgated a view of *dhyana* which differed sharply from the generally accepted practice.⁵

In fact, two centuries had elapsed before the advent of a Zen school in China, with the subsequent founding of Zen monasteries.

The Theory

Curiously, it is by no means clear to which Buddhist term the English word "meditation" corresponds, though *yoga* and the older, specifically Buddhist technical term *bhavana* gain visibility as the two main candidates. Buddhist tradition has come to consider meditation by way of two different yet complementary aspects:

> The two fundamental types of meditation are *samatha* and *vipassana*. The former concentrates on mindfulness of body, feelings, mind and mental states and aims at detaching the mind from responses to sense stimuli through four stages of *jhana* (Sanskrit *dhyana*), which is meditation, until the level of pure consciousness of *samadhi* is achieved, then beyond *samadhi* to four formless states where dualities cease to exist. *Vipassana* or "insight" meditation is more psycho-analytically based, analysing the nature of the self in the context of the fundamental tenets of Buddhism.⁶

Perhaps no section of the Buddha's teaching has been more misunderstood than his words on *bhavana*, which is best translated "culture" or "development". The reference is to the bringing into being, by means of mental or spiritual exercises, of wholesome mental states conducive to the realization of the Buddhist path. Buddhism is a mind-culture, and the purpose of meditation is to cultivate an attitude of mind; it has nothing to do with turning one's back on life and sitting in isolated splendour while in some form of mystical trance or the like. So little understood was the Buddha's teaching on meditation, that at one time it degenerated into a ritual of burning candles and reciting formulae.[7] Great Master Tendo Nyojo once said:

> Learning meditation is to cast off body and mind. It is not necessary to burn incense, prostrate oneself, recite the name of the Buddha, perform repentance or chant sutras. If you concentrate on meditation, your main purpose will be attained.[8]

The Buddha taught that the pre-Buddhist form of meditation known as *samatha* was mind-created and did not give insight into the Ultimate Reality. Although the Buddha did not eschew *samatha* from Buddhist meditation, he nevertheless considered it to have limited value. For the Buddha, the aim of meditation is to effectuate the attainment of highest wisdom that alone recognizes the True Reality and brings about the realization of Ultimate Truth, *nirvana*. The cultivating process involves the overcoming of all negative and impure thoughts (such as lust, anger, indolence and negativity), and the development of pure and positive qualities (such as concentration, energy and confidence); this is "insight" meditation, *vipassana*, which has as its foundation mindfulness, awareness, vigilance and observation.

The Practice

The Buddha's discourse on meditation, known as the *Satipatthana-sutta*, or "The Setting-up of Mindfulness", has four main sections which direct their attention in turn to our body *(kaya)*, feelings and sensations *(vedana)*, the mind *(citta)* and, lastly, moral and intellectual subjects *(dhamma)*. In every instance, being mindfully aware of what is happening at the present moment is a fundamental principle; "The Mindfulness or Awareness of in-and-out breathing" *(anapanasati)* is a case in point. Seated in a specified (by the text) posture, with legs crossed and body erect, the meditator is enjoined to become mindfully aware of an action which we, of necessity, do all the time – breathing in and breathing out. Although one of the simplest practices, it is one which in time will develop considerable powers of concentration and reap all its attendant benefits, even the realization of *nirvana*. The key word here is "develop", for, at first, the mind will flit here and there and do anything other than concentrate on one's breathing; as always, the ego will be determined that it and nothing else, remains the centre of attention.

By the same token, forgetting ourselves completely and losing ourselves in what we are doing also enhances mental development, a fact that has not escaped the attention of Zen Buddhists today. To a detached observer, however, it would appear that so many of us almost crave an out-of-body experience, so determined are we to concentrate on anything other than the task-in-hand. Rather than apply ourselves totally to what we are doing at the present moment, we would far prefer to deliberate over the past and anticipate the future, in dejected or enthusiastic tones, dependent upon our mood. All too often, we find ourselves resentful of the task-in-hand (even if that "task" is having to take time out to meditate!) because this is preventing us from tackling our next assignment. Accordingly, we direct our attention not to what we are doing presently, but to the next task, and when we eventually do that, to the next, and so on. This frenetic behaviour leads nowhere other than to frustration and, far from evolving, the mind resembles some farmyard dog restrained by a chain, that surges furiously first this way and then that, without ever making any real progression.[9]

The theme of an agitated mind is recurrent in Zen. Much of the problem is one of ego, whereby we are convinced that only we know what is really important, and so we place unbelievable strain upon ourselves, rushing through those chores we believe to be less important, like eating properly and spending time with those we love, so that we can get on with that which we alone know to be all-important, meeting that next target. Once the restless mind is weaned away from this treadmill of ignorance, through Right Mindfulness and Right Concentration, it can come to terms with the Buddha's teaching that there is no permanent unchanging self (anatta), anymore than anything can be said to be permanent or unchanging (anicca).

With this realization, belief in an ego that has to be satiated constantly becomes vacuous. This is no easy task, however, and can be accomplished only with regular daily practice and perseverance. This lack of subjectivity is also advocated in the texts when they come to discuss the association between meditation and the mind. Observing the state of mind we are in at any given time, as the mind meanders its way through its galaxy of mood swings, embracing in turn both positive and negative thoughts, should be done objectively and dispassionately. As a scientist views a subject-study without passion, so should we observe our minds, without pride or criticism, and without any thought of having ownership of the anger, worry or love, which becomes voiced in the words, "my worry" or "I am worried". With such a detached view, we become able to analyse the reasons why the emotion in question is dominating our thoughts and act accordingly. At this juncture, it is important to recognize that attachment and fixation have no place in Zen, for the way of Zen is a way of freedom, as Suzuki noted:

> If there is anything Zen strongly emphasizes it is the attainment of freedom; that is, freedom from all unnatural encumbrances. Meditation is something artificially put on; it does not belong to the natural activity of the mind. Upon what do the fowl of the air meditate? Upon what do the fish in the water meditate? They fly; they swim. Is not that enough? . . . there is no object in Zen upon which to fix the thought. Zen is a wafting cloud in the sky. No screw fastens it, no string holds it; it moves as it lists. *No amount of meditation will keep Zen in one place.* Meditation is not Zen.[10]

Nevertheless, for Zen master Dogen the practice of *zazen* and the realization of Buddhahood are synonymous, and Dogen's impact on *zazen* continues to this day. Indeed, more than any other person, Dogen, who introduced Soto Zen to Japan from China, may be described as "the master of *zazen*". Correct posture and breathing are all important, and much has been written on these issues, both then and now.[11] Among all the Zen schools, each with its own ideas on spiritual training, meditation in the posture in which Sakyamuni "awakened" remains to this day the chief path to enlightenment (Jap. *satori*). This said, there are Zen *sanghas* today that acknowledge that the recognized meditative posture is not possible for everyone, and advocate the so-called *chrysanthemum* position, wherein one adopts the most comfortable position, regardless of protocol.

Zazen

Zazen literally means "sitting in meditation", a technical term for the primary practice in all the schools of Zen. Since it is practised in Zen monasteries for several hours each day (and much longer during the intensified training periods known as *sesshin*), *zazen* is often punctuated by periods of walking meditation known as *kinhin*. Meditation in Zen Buddhism is essentially concerned with addressing the questions, "Who am I?" "What am I" and "Why am I the way I am?" This is the essence of meditation. However, the answers to these questions are not to be found by examining theories of the self, or theories of human nature, but by personal encounter. The problem is that this encounter is made difficult by an ego that, through constant chatter, demands attention and directs our thoughts away from that which is real.

Indeed, Dogen himself recognized the dangers of consciously using meditation as a means to strive for Buddhahood. Meditation in Zen is not a question of striving or holding on, but of letting go of thought patterns that seduce us and separate us from reality. Formal meditation, *zazen*, starts the day for the Zen Buddhist with the express purpose of grounding oneself. Accordingly, as thoughts arise naturally in *zazen* so are they allowed to go as easily and quickly as they come; we do not allow our thoughts to develop by going from one thought to another. With thoughts from external stimuli not allowed to come to fruition, rather than looking out at the world around us, we tend to look inwards, *directly pointing to the mind, directly pointing to the human heart*, and in so doing we gain direct experience of our Buddha-nature.

Kensho

> The ego cannot lose itself, it sometimes just gets lost. The practitioner is overcome by emptiness in much the same way, one may suppose, as a blackbird is overcome by its song. Such rare moments are known as "enlightenment experiences".[12]

When the normal flow of conscious thought is interrupted and the senses no longer inform the mind, a state of bliss is attained which has been described as being "outside one's self": this is enlightenment, the ultimate goal of Buddhism, which Zen calls *satori*. Beyond intellect and conceptual thought, this indescribable state, in which one awakens to the Buddha-nature within, is one where all dualities cease, and no subject–object differentiation exists, since the common notion that there is an "I" which has to be appeased and satiated no longer obtains. Once Sakyamuni's insight into the concept of "No-I" becomes internalized, the vista that lies before us is the realization that everything in the cosmos is the Buddha-nature. This is the Ultimate Reality and Truth. With this intuitive realization, this awakening to the Ultimate Truth, comes the dawning that, since the egoistic self is unreal, so the fears that become attached to that which is unreal are vacuous, as are all forms of attachment. As the website at Throssel Hole Priory confirms:

> In meditation, one learns how to accept oneself and the world as it is. Profound transformation becomes possible once we realise this. If I believe that I am separate from everyone else, then I act selfishly to get what I want. If I know that within diversity nothing is separate, then I

already have all I need, for I am One with all things. Meditation enables us to discover the real nature of our own being, to know things as they are.[13]

The danger of failing to recognize this all-important fact is illumined by Ken Jones:

> Antithetical bonding is the mainspring of samsaric history. It is socially constructed delusion. It is group bonding which affirms and exalts belongingness-identity by emphasising the differences and otherness of another group or groups, which are opposed and possibly subordinated. The antithesis may be economic, political, ethnic, religious or, most persistently, by gender. History very much revolves around "us" and "them". And "they" provide a legitimised and often well-researched target for the projection of all the personal fear, anger and self-aversion of which we may be scarcely aware. Once set in train, polarisation and antagonism feed off one another in a tightening spiral. The middle ground is excluded, and tight loyalty to one side or the other is demanded.[14]

There are writers who use the terms *satori* and *kensho* interchangeably, with some justification, since, semantically, both words have the same meaning. Generally speaking, however, the use of *satori* is reserved for the ultimate spiritual experience, whilst *kensho* describes the "entering of the first gate", that is an initial incomplete awakening. The usual English rendering of *kensho* (Chin. *chien-hsing*) is "to see one's true nature"; in other words, 'It is the sudden realization that "I have been complete and perfect from the very beginning. How wonderful, how miraculous."'[15] There is always the danger that *kensho* may be confused with altered or even bizarre states of consciousness, a danger that is readily addressed by the master. Zen masters have also noticed a gender difference in attitudes to *kensho*. Women seem interested to ponder and wonder over its implications, while men have a propensity to view *kensho* as a goal to be achieved.

In theory, *satori* and enlightenment are identical, but in practice not all Zen Buddhists would credit *satori* with this distinction. There are those who would equate *satori* with the Indian *samadhi* which is achieved in deep meditation, without being considered to be enlightenment itself, believing that full Buddhahood lies beyond *satori*. Given the paradoxical nature of Zen, perhaps it is unsurprising that there is disagreement:

> Therefore, without disparaging the significance of Zen enlightenment for earnest Zen disciples, we are driven to question its claim to be the norm

of truth. Furthermore, as a mystical phenomenon, the *satori* experience is imperfect. No human effort to attain enlightenment, no matter how honest and self-sacrificing, can ever lead to the perfect truth.[16]

Soto Zen

The Soto Zen school (Chin. Tsao-tung) is the oldest surviving school of the Zen tradition. Its emphasis is that all beings have the Buddha-nature, and that training and enlightenment are indivisible. The teaching operates within the framework of the Buddhist Precepts, not as an imposition but for anyone wishing to partake of their own free will. Each spring, the Tradition of Serene Reflection Meditation (the Soto Zen school in the West) holds a retreat known as the Keeping of the Ten Precepts. Here, those becoming lay Buddhists formally take the Ten Precepts as outlined in Great Master Dogen's text, *Kyojukaimon (Giving and Receiving the Teaching of the Precepts)*[17]

Do not kill.
Do not steal.
Do not covet.
Do not say that which is not true.
Do not sell the wine of delusion.
Do not speak against others.
Do not be proud of yourself and devalue others.
Do not be mean in giving either Dharma or wealth.
Do not be angry.
Do not defame the Three Treasures (the Buddha, the Sangha and the Dharma).

Germane to these are the Three Pure Precepts which are,

Cease from evil. By refraining from that which causes confusion and suffering, the Truth will shine of itself.
Do only good. Doing good arises naturally from ceasing to do evil.
Do good for others. To cease from evil is to devote one's life to the good of all living things.[18]

By practising *zazen*, and being aware of the Three Pure Precepts, the three grenades (defilements) of greed, anger and delusion diminish naturally. It is not a question of will power or the rote learning of more rules. Doing only good, particularly for others, awakens the heart of compassion in ourselves. At the same time, it is necessary to examine what it is that we do that causes suffering and to cease from this. When suffering is caused by extraneous (such as social or work) pressures, how we respond to these is all-important. There are those who have noted that, metaphysically, the identification and separation of "good" and "evil" introduces duality into what is essentially a non-dual Buddhist system, an objection admirably addressed by Reverend Master Jiyu-Kennett:

> Perfect faith is always changing and always the same, always interesting and always joyful, never seeing an opposite because it has indeed gone beyond opposites. Opposites can only exist when we have not yet transcended them; when they have been transcended every day is a good day, as Keizan says, and all work is the work of the Buddha. At this time there is no such thing as good and bad, like and dislike; there is only the positivity that lies *beyond* these opposites.[19]

Monks and monasteries

> I wish to find the truth. I wish to become one with the eternal, and so sitting down in meditation is a statement of that.
>
> Reverend Master Daishin Morgan

Despite Suzuki's affirmations to the contrary, and his preoccupation with the paradoxical and irrational, meditation is the heart of Zen. But this is not restricted to *zazen*. Both within and without the monastery walls, the intention is to enable meditative practice to embrace each and every action in order to become grounded in yourself, being totally at one with what you are doing at the time, and not frantically trying to keep pace with a mind that is forever fantasizing about the future or bemoaning the past. Driving to work or peeling the vegetables is just as conducive to meditative practice as monastic life. Even in the monastery itself, meditation is not confined to *zazen*. This alternates with participation in manual work as well as religious ceremonies, but always being mindfully aware of the task in hand.

In earlier times, when most people could not read, the enactment of ceremonies was far more meaningful than the scriptures. Even today, ceremonies have great value. At the naming ceremony for babies, the newly born will be offered the protection of buddhas and ancestors, as its head is sprinkled with water. At a Soto Zen wedding ceremony, the bride and groom will adhere to British custom, but each will hold their own burning candle, and light a large third candle before symbolically extinguishing their own. Funeral ceremonies are held in all parts of the country since, as in all forms of Japanese Buddhism, death is held to be the most important life-cycle rite. In death the deceased is considered *to be* Buddha, and it is here that the concept of *letting go*, so fundamental to Zen, is emphasized. Not only do the bereaved need to be assured that it is right and necessary to let go of their loved one, but the deceased also needs to have extinguished the fires of greed, anger and delusion. Should one of these (in any manifestation whatever) remain at the point of death, then it will reappear in the next rebirth (in whatever form that may take).

An Introduction to Throssel Hole Buddhist Abbey attests a typical schedule for those wishing to experience an introductory retreat at the abbey (Friday afternoon until Sunday afternoon):

6 am	Rising	2.15	Working meditation
6.20	Meditation	4.00	Tea/class
6.55	Morning Service	5.00	'Midday' service and meditation
7.59	Temple clean-up	6.00	Medicine meal; the Buddha decreed that *medicine* is allowed at certain times, providing it requires no mastication
8.30	Breakfast, taken formally	6.30	Rest and recollection
9.00	Spiritual reading, the *Kyojukaimon*	7.25	Meditation
10.30	Tea		Walking meditation
11.45	Meditation		Meditation
12.30	Lunch		Evening Office
1.00	Rest/recollection	9.00	Tea
		10.00	Lights out

The work period may consist of cooking, gardening or building work, in short, whatever needs doing. During week retreats and weekend retreats for more experienced meditators, *zazen* will feature more prominently, while during an extensive period of intensive *zazen* known as *sesshin* (a technical term, literally meaning "to collect the mind") everything will take second place to sitting meditation, *including sleep*.

In Soto Zen, ceremonial bowings during group "sitting" are particularly prominent and possibly reflect something of the old Chinese order and grace of Confucianism in the distant beginnings of Zen. The outcome of this extremely simple and straightforward practice is the realization that everyone has the Buddha-nature to which we are inseparably connected, and the act of bowing that permeates monastic life is recognition of this. Bowing also transcends the intellect, since its purpose and function cannot be rationalized intellectually. Bowing is also an expression of gratitude in as much as through meditation we are able to find the source of Truth. This recognition of the importance of bowing is expressed in a saying peculiar to the Soto Zen school:

As long as bowing lasts, Buddhism will last.

Monasteries are for those wishing to dedicate themselves to the spiritual life. The true monastery is the heart, and the monastic life is not mandatory for all Zen Buddhists since, in this light, the monastery is anywhere and everywhere; nor is there any suggestion that the monk (Jap. *unsui*, "free as the clouds") is in some way superior to the lay Buddhist, nor that he or she has a deeper awareness of Buddha-nature. Some simply feel that practice within the monastic tradition is the right way for them while others don't. Both monastic and lay traditions have long and successful histories, and have proved good bedfellows.

Throssel Hole Priory was not purpose built, but traditionally monasteries are constructed in human form, with the *zendo* the heart of the monastery. The ceremony hall is the "head" of the monastery and, as such, would point towards the Pole Star, held to be the unmoving centre of the universe in Chinese tradition. At Throssel Hole, the ceremony hall has an image of Sakyamuni Buddha seated on an altar, before whom offerings of light, incense, flowers, water and fruit are made. The compassion of the Buddha-nature is represented by images of Kwannon (Chin. Kwanyin) and Avalokitesvara, the bodhisattva of compassion (Jap. Kanzeon). The *zendo* has Manjusri, the bodhisattva of wisdom seated on a lion, representing the ego, filled with false pride and full of its own importance. We should not lose sight of the fact that in all forms of Zen Buddhism the starting point is control of the mind.

The head temple of the Soto Zen school in Japan is Eiheiji. It lies some 3000 feet up in the mountains of central Japan. This 700 year old wooden monastery is constructed on different levels, connected by a series of staircases made from cedar wood The novice monk has a six foot by three foot area on a raised platform on which novitiate monks meditate and sleep in the meditation hall or *zendo*; this is literally the monk's home. Accordingly, concern and consideration for others sharing the hall is at a premium. The silence of the *zendo* is shattered at 4.30 a.m. each day by a novitiate bell-ringer, who bows to each arising monk in turn as they pass him on their way to the washroom. Returning to the *zendo*, now wearing ankle length black robes, the monks begin the day with *zazen*, formal meditation, with the intention of grounding oneself, a grounding which is reinforced throughout the day by work, meditation and ceremonies, which give the day a contemplative feel. A wide bench surrounds the *zendo*, upon which the monk sits himself on a black cushion known as a *zafu*.

Appropriately, in the West the Soto Zen school is called Serene Reflection Meditation, a meditative practice wherein the meditator simply *lets go* of any thoughts that arise without allowing them to develop. It's rather like a young man seeing girls go by and watching them as he would passing clouds. Settling down onto his *zafu*, the monk places the left palm of his hand upon his right, with both thumbs touching. The practitioner next positions the tip of his tongue behind his top front teeth, inhaling and exhaling sharply, before returning to a normal breathing pattern.

Letting go is the essence of monastic life. As surely as the monk lets go of arising thoughts, so must the world itself be renounced. But this is a gradual process that cannot be achieved in one fell swoop; the physical move from urban culture to monastic retreat is the easy part, renouncing emotions, fixed-views, opinions and prejudices that are in the very depths of one's being is far more difficult. Perhaps the weekly shaving of the head is a gentle reminder that the act of renunciation is a gradual, but ongoing thing. Nor must it be assumed that because the Buddhist's aim is to go beyond suffering, and the monk is aware of how he or she should respond to internal and social causes, monks are spared the mental anguish that torments us all; indeed, the more one becomes aware of and compassionate towards others' pain, the more one suffers for them.

It is a common mistake to see meditation as some form of escapism, with the meditator who stares at the wall intentionally facing in that direction so as to turn his or her back on the world and all its problems. But there is nowhere to hide in the monastery, nor, indeed, in meditation, for one cannot hide from oneself. With extraneous thoughts not allowed to come to fruition, one comes face-to-face with oneself and all one's personality problems . . . a sobering thought indeed:

So the way through that inner landscape entails penetrating and dissolving all the encrustations on that human heart that is smothered by my lusts, greed, fears, hatreds, my stubbornness, opinions, notions, assumptions, passionate beliefs and assertions, my longings and aversions which together make up my dissatisfaction with what is.[20]

As surely as meditation is said to be the heart of Zen, so the monastery itself has a pulse, a heartbeat that pumps its lifeblood away from the heart and returns it to the source, the heart of meditation. In a monastery that is functioning perfectly, with every action of every meditator performed as an act of meditation, then the monastery itself becomes an expression of the mind of meditation. Hubert Benoit cites a Zen dialogue between a Master and a monk that illustrates well the difference between the working world of the ordinary person and the working meditation of the monk:

MONK:	*'Is there a special way of working in the Tao?'*
MASTER:	*'Yes, there is.'*
MONK:	*'What is it?'*
MASTER:	*'When you are hungry, eat; when you are tired, sleep.'*
MONK:	*'That is what everyone does; so is their way the same as yours?'*
MASTER:	*'It is not the same.'*
MONK:	*'Why not?'*
MASTER:	*'When they eat they do not simply eat, their minds are busy with all kinds of imagination; when they sleep they do not simply sleep, they give free rein to a thousand idle thoughts. That is why their way is not my way.'*[21]

This kind of mindfulness is a hallmark of much Buddhist tradition, from the practices of Theravada to Soto Zen "sitting": underpinning it is the egoless mind and the need to still the mind from *karma* producing desires, aversions, cravings and the differentiation of things in life which give a distorted picture of reality.

But Soto Zen extends far beyond the *zendo*, indeed far beyond the monastery walls. Lay Buddhists may support the monastery financially but Throssel Hole Priory supports the lay Buddhists spiritually, for it is also a training centre. Some thirty groups throughout the country meet regularly and follow the teachings of Throssel Hole. The advice given to lay Buddhists is to establish a regular twice-daily pattern of meditation, with regularity being far more important than duration; meditation is not an endurance feat. Whenever possible, meditation within a group situation is encouraged. As with the monks, the emphasis is on being mindful, mindful of the task in hand rather than fretting over what also needs doing. The power of this practice is not diminished by location, for you can be just as mindful of walking the dog in the park as working for the monastery within its confines.

The practice of *zazen*, or sitting meditation, is central to all forms of Zen, but in Soto Zen it is the most important factor. There are no frenetic interchanges with Zen Masters or meditating on *koans*, for it is simply *sitting*, termed *shikantaza*, which is the main practice. The Soto Zen method of meditation is perhaps the most natural of all forms of meditation, for there is no need to use *mantras* or to focus the attention on *mandalas*. The Buddhist simply sits on his or her chair or low stool (termed a "bench") or on the floor, with a straight back and facing a blank wall. The eyes remain open but focused down, following the line of the nose to a point on the wall a foot or so above the floor. When thoughts arrive in the mind, they are simply brushed aside and passed away without allowing them to develop. So as the sounds of the immediate environment filter into the mind, the mind does not react to them. Or, when the events of the day or previous day, or the concerns for the remainder of the day come to mind, the mind softly brushes them aside. The mind, then, is not allowed to think; thoughts are not allowed to develop. In this case, the mind is able to become tranquil and the Buddha-nature, which is beneath the ordinary levels of consciousness and mind processes, is allowed to surface. Soto Zen is a simple, quiet and natural form of Buddhism, even when walking meditation or *kinhin* is interspersed with "sitting". Here, concentration is upon walking in a slow, calm, yet aware manner, traits that foster a greater insight into how one should lead one's life. Soto Zen accepts that the experience of Buddhahood will gradually be awakened, for Buddhahood is already there in each being waiting to be experienced. None of the sudden and dramatic insight of Rinzai Zen is necessary here.

Indeed, the great Rinzai master Hakuin (died 1769) would have none of this "silent-illumination Zen" which he castigated as "dead-sitting". For Hakuin, as indeed for earlier Zen masters, as well as austere patriarchs, a full investigation of the koan device is essential, as is a right understanding of meditation, two points taken up by Western Ch'an today:

> Monks and teachers of eminent virtue, surrounded by hosts of disciples and eminent worthies, foolishly take the dead teachings of no-thought and no-mind, where the mind is like dead ashes with wisdom obliterated,

and make these into the essential doctrines of Zen. They practice silent, dead sitting as though they were incense burners in some old mausoleum and take this to be the treasure place of the true practice of the patriarchs. They make rigid emptiness, indifference, and black stupidity the ultimate essence for accomplishing the Great Matter.[22]

Generally, Zen accepts the non-duality of all things and thereby their total monistic identity. *Nirvana*, therefore, is *samsara* and all beings possess Buddhahood as the Ultimate Reality and are equal to each other. This is beautifully illustrated when in Soto Zen initiation of lay people into the sect, the abbot bows to the lay person who is being initiated, symbolizing the inner equality between the two beings. In the lay ordination ceremony (Jap. *jukai*) the ordinand is given a *ketchimyaku*, a scroll depicting the unbroken line from Sakyamuni to the novitiate's own teacher, having his/her own name added. Having Buddhahood within means that one has to awaken to it – instantly in Rinzai Zen, gradually in Soto Zen – but both accept that each person is already a Buddha, as is every animate and inanimate object. Buddhahood means ultimately the interconnectedness of all within the cosmos, and that the cosmos itself is contained in each being and in every grain of dust.

Zen is not isolated from life, it is life; it is working, eating, cooking, gardening as much as meditating or engaging in spiritual activity, and working meditation is an important dimension of both Rinzai and Soto Zen. Zen Buddhists are not to be found seated in meditation all day long. Most lay Buddhists are in regular employment (though they may well pay a tithe to the monastery) and are engaged in the everyday aspects of life. Effort has to be put into these mundane tasks as much as into meditation in the monastery, but it is a natural effort, not a striving of the self to get rid of the self. The Taoist concept of *wu-wei* in Rinzai Zen means the acquisition of the goal of enlightenment without really aiming for it. There would therefore be no distinction between ordinary, secular existence and the sacred life of a monk. *Satori* can be gained as much through practical activity as through intensive meditation. One Soto Zen Buddhist said of his being assigned to the working meditation of cleaning the Priory during one of his stays at Throssel Hole:

In cleaning the temple I came to realize that you are not cleaning the temple, the temple is cleaning you. And ultimately the temple is pure, and so are you; neither needs cleaning, but I had to clean it to realize it. In such working meditation there is a formal cognitive commitment to the task after which comes an experience of the realization of things as they really are.[23]

This confession echoes the story of someone raking the gravel of a very simple, scarcely ornamented, Zen garden. It took three months to get it right, but on the day that person got it right, there was no need to do it again, insight had occurred. A Ph.D. student I once knew meticulously researched an area of Buddhism for five painstaking years. Upon completion of his doctoral dissertation and when it was due for submission, he slowly walked to the bottom of his garden, gathered together some old newspapers, placed some kindling wood on them and, in the same meticulous manner . . . you don't need me to finish this story.

8 Koan Practice

Tsu-hsin approached the master Hui-nan. As he was about to bow, the master smiled and said: "You have now come into my room." Tsu-hsin was filled with joy and said: "If the truth of Zen is what I now possess, why do you make us swallow all the old stories and exhaust ourselves struggling to make sense of them?" The master said: "If I did not make you struggle in every possible way to discover their meaning, so that you eventually reached a state of no-struggle and no-effort where you could see with your own eyes, I am sure you would forfeit any chance of finding yourself."[1]

The koan (Chin. *kung an*) is a Chinese invention that literally means "public notice or notification", a meaning that has long been all but ignored. Unique to Zen Buddhism, koans are not nonsense. These short, apparently paradoxical riddles, or slightly longer stories posed by the master, sometimes offer the pupil a choice between two possible answers, neither of which is acceptable at face value. As surely as the meaning and purpose of life cannot be resolved by use of the intellect, neither is it possible to solve the meaning of the koan by this means. Since enlightenment cannot be realized by conceptualized thought processes, the koan is employed not to develop powers of conceptualization, but to disrupt the sequence of logical thought and so bring about enlightenment by inducing an altered state of consciousness. In this state, the meanings of all koans will effortlessly be revealed. Scholars have long sought parallels amongst other religions, and the combination of a unique master–pupil relationship, essential for koan practice, and accompanying legendary anecdotes is also to be found in, among others, Hassidic Judaism. It has been argued that the Taoist text, the *Chuan-Tzu*, is a textual koan in the literature of Zen. Although, "such an argument is of necessity historically backwards, since Zen (or Ch'an) arises much later in history . . . it would not be surprising to find that certain characteristics of the child were to be found in the generic make-up of the parent".[2] Nevertheless, it was Martin Buber himself who admitted the koan to be "a genre absolutely peculiar to Zen".

Ruth Fuller Sasaki, an acknowledged authority on the koan, has claimed:

> The koan is not a conundrum to be solved by a nimble wit. It is not a verbal psychiatric device for shocking the disintegrated ego of a student into some kind of stability. Nor, in my opinion, is it ever a paradoxical statement except to those who view it from outside. When the koan is resolved it is realized to be a simple and clear statement made from the state of consciousness which it has helped to awaken.[3]

For Sasaki, koan study is, at one and the same time, systematic and reasonable, a view shared by the Western Ch'an Fellowship. However, her denial of the paradoxical nature of the koan is not shared by all, and D. T. Suzuki was ever fascinated by what he considered to be the irrational and paradoxical character of the koan. Nevertheless, one cannot fail to think of the small child to whom parental decisions are incomprehensible, growing into adulthood and then reflecting on the wisdom of their earlier judgement.

Although the koan is an extremely efficacious device, long associated with the essence of Zen, it must be said that it is not the only means of realizing *satori*, nor is it the most important method, which remains to this day the practice of meditation as exemplified by the Buddha Sakyamuni. The starting point to awakening is taking control of the wandering mind, a mind enmeshed by false thoughts and views as it surfs the world of unreality. The aim is to reveal the pure mind, unsullied by a single thought and, hence, freed from discrimination and discernment.

It is claimed that, long ago, awakening was far simpler to realize than today. Ch'an masters compared the immediacy of the pupils' responses in early days to those of a horse that reacts instantly to the mere sight of a whip. The advance of so-called civilization, however, saw a decline in immediate awakening, and the subsequent introduction of devices that later became known as koans. Such acts included gestures, blows and shouts, as well as words and roars of laughter. The Buddha's awakening of Mahakasyapa by raising a flower, and Bodhidharma's quieting the first Chinese patriarch's mind are examples of a variety of koan devices. Another well-known koan asks, "What is the sound of one hand clapping?" Also, "If you meet someone along the road who has realized the truth, you may not walk past the person in silence, nor speaking. So how should you meet this person?" Koans in the form of short stories include the tale of the goose that grew increasingly large inside a bottle until it was too large to leave. The koan asks how the owner removed the goose from the bottle without harming either.

Such koans, of which there are about 1700, with some 700 in frequent use, are not meant to have any meaning for the unenlightened mind that clings to the names and terms in conditioned human language and perception. Thinking about a koan pushes the mind beyond all logic and intellectualism, producing a tension that brings one to the limits of thought. All the koans arose from the teachings of Zen masters to their pupils, and the records of interchanges between them were gathered and formulated. Frequently, they were based on actual events within the masters' experiences. There is no one "answer" to the koans; individual spontaneity is expected and non-verbal responses are encouraged. Normally associated with the House of Rinzai, the koan is not peculiar to this school; Dogen was introduced to the koan during his stay in China, and though less popular in Soto Zen, the use of koans is not unknown here. Conversely, some eminent Rinzai masters have ignored the use of koans in their teachings, though the efforts of Hakuin Ekaku (1685–1768), who introduced a systematized structure to the classification of koans, offered this method a rejuvenation that has been maintained to the present.

Although a single koan may unlock the door to all other koans, koans are not of one kind; they have been graded into five levels. Case 1 of the *Mumonkan*, "Joshu's *Mu*", is for the student who is beginning. Often said to be the first koan in formal practice, it belongs to the series of koans known as *Hosshin* (ultimate reality), inviting the student to glimpse the Buddha-nature perhaps for the first time, and to recognize its unity and pervasiveness. The next series is known as *Kikan* (support), wherein the distinctiveness of reality is now glimpsed. Next come the *Gonsen* koans (pondering words), an invitation for the student to consider the meanings of the words of the men of old. These are followed by the *Nanto* koans, which require supreme effort by the student to pass through, because of their difficulty. Finally, the student is enjoined to penetrate the series of *Goi* koans, the well-known "Five Ranks", and master the twin defilements of grasping and delusion.

In *zazen*, attention is given at the outset to correct posture and breathing, but concentration may be increased by the introduction of a key word such as "*Mu*" (meaning "nothingness", "empty", "non-being")[4] on which to meditate, and the practitioner who uses this technique transcends dualities in terms of subject–object differentiation and "becomes one with nothing". Zen masters have likened the difficulties of transcending conceptualized thought patterns and the subsequent realization of intuitive knowledge to the chick tapping away at an eggshell from which it needs to escape. Interestingly, this is a view not shared by Western Ch'an, and John Crook notes Master Sheng-yen's argument that, "meditation without conceptual understanding is a very limited activity and that attainment of insight requires both".[5]

The introduction of a koan in the form of a so-called riddle that precludes rational solution is designed to reveal intuitively, through a flash of insight, the Buddha-nature within. The first koan in a collection known as the *Mumonkan* (the Gateless Gate/Barrier), compiled by Mumon Ekai /Wu-men Hui-k'ai (1183–1260) is the most famous and most practised of all. It asks the question, "Has a dog also got Buddha-nature?" to which Master Joshu (Chin. Chao-chou) replies, "*Mu*". Clearly, the monks' question is one that could reasonably be expected to elicit a positive or negative response; equally clearly, this is not the way of the koan, for absolute truth lies beyond affirmation or negation. It is seldom reported that Joshu was asked this self-same question not once, but several times. Nor are we told that he sometimes responded, "Yes" (it does have the Buddha-nature). It has been well said that eastern thought will always remain beyond the compass of western mind and nowhere is this more evident than in recent interpretations given to the first koan in formal study.

Curiously, western writers usually provide an English translation to the above question, but leave the answer in the original tongue, either *Mu* (Jap.) or *Wu* (Chin.). Problems arise when commentators next inform the reader that *Wu/Mu* is best translated "No", and interpret the koan to mean, "A dog does not have Buddha-nature." But this would introduce dualism into an essentially non-dual, Buddhist system and invite the reader to draw the obvious conclusion, that, of course, "humans do have Buddha-nature." It needs only one such writer in an unguarded moment (and there are many who have done so recently) to do this and others quickly follow suit, supposedly establishing pure supposition as well-known fact, with disastrous results. We will do well to remember that because something is well known does not mean to say that it is known well. First-year students at University look at me in total disbelief when I tell them that the most well-known story in so-called western thought, the story of the Nativity, contains no mention of a donkey, no mention of a stable and no mention of *three* wise men,[6] nor are three wise men attested anywhere in the biblical record.

Although the student of the first koan is certainly not being asked to concentrate directly on *nothingness* (the preferred translation of *Mu/Wu*) in a nihilistic sense, the invitation, nevertheless, is to view *Mu* as a meaningless sound, a *yana* or ferry to the other shore of *satori*. For master Wu-men, *Mu/Wu* is the single barrier to the Gate of the Zen school, no effort must be spared, and the practitioner must transcend Non-Being and Being. According to Chung-Ying Cheng, the concept of Non-Being *(wu)* was introduced in the traditions associated with the *Yijing*, traditions that sought to transform the Taoist concept of *Dao* to a metaphysical level. As he points out:

> This innovation and insight consist in introducing the notion of void or non-being *(wu)* into metaphysical thinking on reality and life. In the light of this innovation and insight, the *Yijing* philosophy of *dao* as *taiji* becomes the daoist philosophy of *dao* and *wu*.[7]

Taiji, here, is the indescribable potentiality of a unified source, but, as yet, a *no-thing*.

To accept "Joshu's *Mu*" as a direct answer does violence to its categorization as a koan. Wing-tzit Chan attests to the complexity of the position when he writes:

> There is nothing wrong in rendering *wu* as a negative. However, in some cases it has to be interpreted. For example, *wu-hsin* is not just "no mind" but "no deliberate mind of one's own," and *wu-wei* is not simply "inaction" but "taking no unnatural action," or in Buddhist usage, "not produced from causes."[8]

On this view, to translate *wu* baldly as "No" in the first koan is far too simplistic a rendering unless it is seen as a protest, "No!" against the emptiness of the question. If television courtroom dramas are to be believed, the most frequent directive given to witnesses is, 'Just answer the question, "Yes" or "No"' – an extremely naïve demand, based on the mistaken premise that all questions have legitimacy. We need look no further than the vacuous inquiry, "Do all mermaids die at sea?" to recognize how preposterous this demand can be. Time and again, Sakyamuni Buddha failed to respond to questions that he considered to be without warrant, and it could just be that Joshu's reply was given in the same tone. In this light, Joshu is not to be seen giving a direct reply, but simply rejecting the validity of the "have/have not" question, putting it back to his questioners by pointing out its emptiness.

The legitimacy of this particular question is entirely dependent on accepting the three conditions of "form", "name" and "Being" as integral to the question. Clearly, the questioners' mindset was locked into all three, as introducing the word/name/Being "dog" attests. But the questioners could not see beyond this, could not see beyond "Being", and hence remained in ignorance of that which is beyond "Being" – "Non-Being". Joshu's response "*Mu*" equates in a stroke the Buddha-nature with emptiness (*sunyata*), which is the total opposite of form, name and Being, for it is beyond them, yet it is the emptiness within them. This leaves the practitioner with much over which to ponder. It could well be that Joshu was drawing attention to humankind's obstinate clinging to the forms, names and Being replete in human language and perception. "Even Ananda, who was one of the most intelligent disciples of the Buddha, was reprimanded by the World Honoured One for clinging to names and terms which caused him to neglect self-cultivation".[9] In this light, Joshu's objection is to the naïvety of the question by the introduction of name, form and Being implicit in the word "dog".[10]

Moreover, the great Japanese philosophical thinker, Dogen, emphasized that there can be no question of all sentient beings *having* the Buddha-nature. In his monumental work, the *Shobogenzo*, he makes the point that his reading of the *Mahaparinirvana Sutra* clearly attests that all beings *are* the Buddha-nature. Be this as it may, there is no escaping the fact that, since the Buddha-nature is common to all existence, the question whether all sentient beings (dogs included) either have or do not have the Buddha-nature, is meaningless. Wu-men Hui-k'ai also warned against forming any relative conceptions of "has" or "has not":

> The dog, the Buddha nature,
> The pronouncement, perfect and final.
> Before you say it has or has not,
> You are a dead man on the spot.

The first koan is not an enquiry into "nothingness". Nor is the question of whether a dog has or does not have the Buddha-nature the point at issue; this is not what the practitioner is working on. If it were, and the question is met with the direct response, "No", then one could be forgiven for asking, "So where is the koan?" To suggest that Wu-men Hui-k'ai struggled for six years with a straightforward question accompanied by a direct response beggars belief. "As an object of attention, the koan itself is not of the slightest interest, but what is interesting and effective is its use to drag the attention away from the formal level."[11]

We will do well to remember that the message of the koan is never direct, nor is it the same for every student, nor indeed for the same student returning to the same koan. This is why there can be no definitive "correct" answer to any koan. Indeed, it has been well said that, "it was the process of solving them, rather than their solution, that was most important".[12] To speak of there being a generally acceptable answer to *any* koan infers its being arrived at through the conventional processes of reasoning and deduction. "If, instead of disciplining his mind, a student is urged to stir it in search of the so-called solution to kung ans, he will be turned round by the unending flow of his thoughts and will never be able to pause for a moment to see clearly; he will mistake a robber for his own son, as the masters put it."[13] The way of the koan is to break down logical thought, not promote it, for something beyond logic is involved here. The aim is not to seek answers but to invite the koan to infuse the mind. Not that the mind welcomes this intrusion, for its limited vision is firmly channelled, resisting change at every turn, with *satori* thoroughly obscured from sight.

It is the master who decides whether a student has responded to a particular koan to *his* satisfaction, and may therefore progress to the next stage. Since early times, the master's instruction to the pupil determined the actual form of koan practice; even today, the master will use the same koan in different ways for different students. The message will heighten with the consciousness of the student in the same way that a schoolteacher responds differently to the same question from different cohorts (year groups), and a mother to her children of different ages; the Hindu *Upanisads* make this very point. Accordingly, publications that purport to explain the meanings of koans, and provide answers to each and every one, are vacuous.

Koan practice will vary amongst schools and between masters and pupils. Sometimes the koan will be presented in its entirety, sometimes in part. The practice of summarizing the entire koan in one clue word (sometimes suggested in the koans themselves) is known in Japanese as *jakugo*. Here the koan is reduced to just one word, and the practitioner enjoined to concentrate on it constantly: Joshu's "*Mu*" is a case in point. In Zen literature, this is likened to a man whose mouth holds a red-hot iron ball that he earnestly desires to expectorate, incessantly tossing it from one side of his mouth to the other, because he is unable to do so. Critics of *jakugo* say that it diminishes the purpose and function of the koan, reducing it to little more than an aid to concentration. The constant repetition of the clue word (such as "*Mu*") has been likened to the *nembutsu* of Pure Land Buddhism, where the name of Amida Buddha is continually chanted; D. T. Suzuki never tired of drawing attention to the similarity.

Occasionally, koans could be formed from the *sutras* themselves, more frequently from anecdotes peculiar to the monasteries, or from poignant teachings of the masters. However, from early Chinese beginnings, the favourite source of material for the koan was the *mondo*. Sometimes the "case" of some koans would take the form of a dialogue between master and pupil, engaged in with such rapidity that the sequence of logical thought patterns would be transcended and intuitive knowledge attained instantly. In other cases, exchange need not always be rapid as long as instant intuitive knowledge was gained by the pupil. So, like other aspects of Rinzai Zen, the *mondo* is designed to change normal thinking and knowing in the empirical sense and, in so doing, bring experience of the Buddha-nature within. In his introduction to *Two Zen Classics: Mumonkan and Hekiganroku*, A. V. Grimstone describes well the disciple's approach to koan study:

> We might draw an analogy and say that a collection of koans is like a well-equipped gymnasium in which the Zen student can train himself. He can start with fairly simple exercises and progress to more difficult ones. What he achieves depends on his own efforts. The gymnasium is useless unless he gets to work in it.[14]

Heinrich Dumoulin observed that we will never know the actual form that shaped koan practice in early times, while Thomas Cleary notes that the failure of offshoots of Japanese and Korean Zen to understand the structure of the koan tended to present the koan as a form of mystery cult.[15] Even today, the precise purpose and function of the koan remain unclear, and its use and abuse by both writers and sixties dropouts such as hippies and beatniks, with their attendant drug problems, brought nothing but discredit to both Zen in general and the koan in particular. Nevertheless, amidst all the confusion and misunderstanding, some genuine, some deliberate, it is possible to discern a kernel of truth:

> The koan, as understood in Zen Buddhism, consciously or unconsciously includes a moment of questioning and doubt. The Zen practitioner is a seeker who turns for guidance and help to the master. The experienced, creative master is able to give the disciple the answer appropriate to him, which is imprinted indelibly on the questioner's memory. From this initial situation, we must suppose, the koan arose.[16]

The arresting, terse retorts of the esteemed Rinzai masters, designed to create a tension that in turn would bring about an altered state of consciousness, were soon in circulation amongst the disciples, and Suzuki went so far as to say: "To my mind it was the technique of the koan exercise that saved Zen as a unique heritage of Far eastern culture." Finally, and with apologies to Winston Churchill, we may definitely conclude of the koan device:

"It is *not* a riddle wrapped in a mystery inside an enigma."

9 The Master–Pupil Relationship

A special transmission outside the scriptures;
No dependence upon words and letters;
Direct pointing to the mind;
Seeing into one's own nature and realizing Buddhahood.

This verse of unknown composition, generally assigned to the Tang dynasty in China, is of fundamental importance to an understanding of Zen; at the same time, if taken at face value, it raises more questions than it answers. Few would disagree that central to Zen teaching is the ability "to see one's true nature" (the usual English rendering of *kensho*), but what of the assertion that there should be "no dependence upon words and letters"? If this is so, and we read between the lines, then it appears that it is not only the scriptures that can be dispensed with, but the master–pupil relationship itself. Clearly, this is a question that deserves closer examination.

Rather than reading *between* the lines, it may be prudent to begin by reading the lines themselves, and consider what they say. Nowhere does the verse suggest that words and letters have no value in Buddhist thought, rather the affirmation is that they should not be *depended* upon. When the Buddha Sakyamuni became dissatisfied with the instruction he had received from the celebrated forest hermits and teachers, he sought enlightenment without their help. Having, at last, realized this state, he overcame the (final) temptation to keep his own counsel, and resolved to offer other seekers of truth a prescription for their own transformation. It was this resolve that heralded the Buddhist tradition of spiritual guidance. Insofar as the Buddha was not so much a teacher as a physician, the term "prescription" is entirely apposite. No responsible doctor would write the same prescription for every patient, and the teaching should always be appropriate to the level of consciousness of the audience; accordingly, contradictory teachings must have arisen.[1].

Consider the famous Fire Sermon; a father is devastated to find his house ablaze upon his return home, particularly since his three children are within. Try as he might, he cannot attract their attention, mainly due to the fact that they are of different ages and engrossed in their own private worlds. He next varies his approach, concentrating on the youngest first. He produces a suitable toy that would have appealed to the youngster, and the child emerges. This has no effect whatever on the other children, so he next attracts the attention of the middle child by displaying a toy appropriate to his age range; this child also comes to the father. Finally, the eldest child emerges with a third change of (appropriate) toy. As surely as the children are *drawn out* of the inferno by appealing to their levels of consciousness, so does Buddhist teaching vary according to the level of consciousness of the audience. In so doing, it is their inner wisdom that is *drawn out*.

Far from viewing the Buddha as divine, or even as an intermediary to the divine, early Buddhism saw Sakyamuni as very much a mortal who ceased to exist once he had entered mortality:

> early Buddhism emphasized the humanity of the guide and his own attainment of spiritual knowledge. The term designated by the texts for the guide or teacher is "good or virtuous friend" (Pali, *kalyanamitta*; Skt. *kalyanamitra*). The *kalyanamitra* provides guidance based entirely on the insight he has gained from personal experience. In one instance the *Samyutta Nikaya* reports that when Ananda suggested to the Buddha that reliance on "virtuous friends" was half the holy life, the Buddha corrected him by declaring it the whole of holy life.[2]

It is said that, above all else, the function of the Zen master is to produce a disciple capable of transmitting the *dharma*, hence preserving the lineage. Failure to produce worthy disciples has resulted in many lineages becoming extinct after a generation or two. Long ago, Atisa (died 1054) likened the breaking of the chain of transmission to the transformation of the scriptures into a broken corpse, which nothing can revitalize. The origin of the tradition that began with Sakyamuni and is transmitted through the lineage via the master–pupil relationship finds expression in the chanting of the ancestral line each morning in all Soto Zen monasteries. Tradition has it that the smile of realization that dawned on the face of Mahakasyapa when the Buddha raised the flower all those years ago also heralded the dawn of Zen Buddhism. So began the transmission of the *Mind Dharma*, the beginning of the master–pupil relationship that spans twenty-five centuries and is of fundamental importance to Zen. The master is held in deep respect as the incumbent representative of Sakyamuni, and his purpose is not to introduce a new teaching but to point the way to one's Buddha-nature. Accordingly, our understanding must be our own, not the revelation of others. We saw earlier that this is why the thirteenth-century compiler of the Mumonkan wrote, "When you meet the Buddha you kill him; when you meet the patriarchs you kill them." For Wu-men Hui-k'ai, it is the illusory, discriminating mind that sets up its own barriers to *satori*, obscuring the Buddha-nature and creating duality or nihilism.

Sakyamuni was convinced that his personal experience of enlightenment had revealed to him the *dharma*, the universal law of existence, and it was this belief that gave Buddha his authority. For Sakyamuni, the *dharma* was the sole guiding principle of life, a conviction that he urged his disciples to adopt and follow. But this was not a self-evident truth; rather it was one that was entirely dependent on the primacy of self-knowledge. With the acceptance of the primacy of personal experience came a general trend away from scriptural study. Although there certainly was a place for the Buddhist canon, study of the traditional scriptures began to occupy very much a second place in importance to the Mahayana in general and Zen in particular.

> A scripture is considered useful insofar as it can lead one to the same religious experience that the Buddha himself had during his life. The implication is that scriptures can ultimately be dispensed with.[3]

It has been well said that experience cannot be accurately or adequately conveyed to one who has not experienced it. Personal experience is everything in Zen. A writer once told his Zen Buddhist friend that he had been commissioned to write about Zen. His friend congratulated him and invited him to spend a weekend in retreat at a monastery. Thanking him for his kindness, the writer objected, "But it's not experience I want; it's information." His friend then told him something he should have already known, "But they go together." The writer was being offered first-hand experiential knowledge, which is the only way to understand Zen, but he failed to recognize this. Being a writer, words were all-important to him, for his brief was to write about Zen Buddhism. In his view, his approach should be intellectual, but such an approach can only be made from a position of unreality. This is not to deride intellect, but to affirm that the starting point must be an experiential one; only when this foundation is established may the intellect be gainfully employed. Suzuki went so far as to say, "to study Zen means to have Zen experience, for without the experience there is no Zen one can study".[4]

Reverend Master Daishin Morgan, abbot at Throssel Hole Priory, observes that Zen Buddhism is less dependent than some other traditions upon the written form. A student of mine once needed to know the textual source of the Four Noble Truths in the *Sutta Pitaka*. When he was invited by a Zen friend to the Festival of Wesak, he saw this as a golden opportunity to attain this knowledge. During lunch he determined to ask those present, and was surprised to learn that the first Buddhists he asked didn't know. After asking more and more Buddhists and receiving a negative response each time, he realized he would have to ask the monks (in Soto Zen, men and women are called "monks"). To his complete astonishment, he gradually came to realize that no one in the entire *sangha* could answer his question, nor did anyone consider it to be a particularly interesting question. Although there is no single authoritative Buddhist canon recognized by every school, the Zen canon is the largest of all. For Zen, however, there is no single text, ritual or practice that is observed by every Zen disciple. As one Zen master illumined, "Awakening is the rule".

In Zen thought, mankind lacks *nothing* other than the need to awaken to the fact. It is like a block of ice in man which has all the properties of water and needs only the generation of heat in order for these properties to become manifest. Zen masters over the centuries have addressed the question of how best to awaken their students, sometimes subtly, sometimes not so subtly, to this awareness. Until her death on November 6 1996, the head and source of the Soto Zen order in Britain (now known as the Order of Buddhist Contemplatives) was Reverend Master Jiyu-Kennett. Invited to Japan in 1962 to train as disciple with the chief abbot of of one of Japan's principal monasteries, she was ordained as a Buddhist monk *en route* to Malaysia. Here she was given the Chinese equivalent of her name, Sumitra (Jap. Jiyu: True Friend). The eventual demise of the chief abbot saw her return to the West in 1969 as a Zen master. Here, she founded not only Throssel Hole Priory in Northumberland, but also Shasta Abbey in California, where she lived out her life. A musician, she transposed the Buddhist sutras to music and the resultant effect of chanting in plainsong is quite exquisite to the ear.

Although there will always be a master–pupil relationship, in the strictest sense of the term, the fulfilment of this spiritual relationship will foster a realization of the emptiness of *both* parties. The role of the master has been likened to that of the helper who gives his arm in support of the novice swimmer. As soon as the pupil is an able swimmer, it is the master's *duty* to withdraw his support, lest it becomes a crutch. No matter how skilled the driving instructor, and how inexperienced the pupil, once the pupil has passed the driving test, the skills of the instructor are superfluous, leaving the pupil free to continue to drive the road of experience. As surely as the raft is no longer required once the far shore is reached, the need for the master is impermanent. Thomas Cleary also notes that, "Offshoots of Korean and Japanese sects, not understanding the structure of the koans, have tended to make this aspect of Zen into a cult of secrecy, mystery, and/or simple mystification."[5] If this is so, then this misunderstanding opens the door to further confusion, with the need for a master to unravel these supposed "mysteries" that are to the fore of practitioners' minds. Nor must we become attached to the master by virtue of the esteem in which he is held.

In some Buddhist traditions – Tantra is a case in point – the master's word carries absolute authority, and if the pupil does not understand what it is that his master advises (or, rather, *why* this advice is being given), this is because his level of consciousness is deemed to be lower than that of the master. Absolute trust in the master finds manifestation in total devotion and obedience, for the lamas (Tibetan gurus) are the embodiment of emptiness. The Venerable Geshe Damcho Yonten, resident lama at Lam Rim Tibetan Buddhist Centre at Raglan, Monmouthshire made a salient point when he said, "Emptiness is not enlightenment, enlightenment is the all-knowing of everything." It is not without significance that the title "Dalai Lama" (the spiritual head of Tibetan Buddhism) means "Ocean" (of knowledge). Utter devotion to the master in Tantric Buddhism symbolizes the close relationship between the self (form) and the lama (emptiness). In attempts to overcome the self-imposed fetters of greed, anger and delusion (that comprise the ego), newcomers to Tantric Buddhism, who have admitted an aversion to meat or alcohol, have been instructed to partake of the same on a regular basis. Tantric Buddhists who have disobeyed their master have been asked to leave the order, since the master always knows best. *This is not the way of Zen.*

Reverend Master Jiyu-Kennett distinguishes between absolute faith and perfect faith. Absolute faith, by definition, demands absolute obedience to the master. Perfect faith, on the other hand, invites a refreshing freedom of mind. Here, it is not a question of blind obedience to the master, but one of give and take, *with the master just as willing to learn as the pupil*. We will do well to remember this. Some time ago I was speaking with a young student who happened to enquire what I enjoyed doing in my spare time. I explained that I love learning and that it is my sincere wish that I should be in a position to learn something even on the day that I die. "Oh, but you will be!" he assured me. Seeing my puzzled look, he added, "You will learn what's on the other side" . . . the young student was eight years old!

> However humble a person may appear to be, if this desire (to save all living beings) has been awakened, he is already the teacher of all mankind: a little girl of seven even may be the teacher of the four classes of Buddhists and the mother of True Compassion to all living things.[6]

Joan Baez once said, "All of us are looking for the guru. And at the same time you know *the* guru has to be a phony."[7] Since none of us want to suffer, and since there is the possibility of meeting someone who can alleviate our suffering, perhaps inwardly we all seek a guru. When the said master does not live up to expectations, however, this can be devastating. We need look no further than the case of Dr Harold Shipman to see the utter devastation that can be caused by placing unquestioning trust in someone, simply because that person is in a position of authority. On 31 January 2000 the Manchester G.P. was convicted on 15 counts of murder. Since qualifying as a doctor, it is believed that this much loved physician poisoned hundreds of his patients who entrusted themselves to his care, using morphine or diamorphine (heroin) to administer death. This would make Shipman the most prolific serial killer the world has known. Hardly a month goes by without our reading about some Christian priest or other who has disgraced himself, abusing the power and authority that have been invested in him, to satisfy his own evil ends. But this is a so-called Christian country, so we would hear more about such "Christian" misdemeanours than the weaknesses of other faith leaders. We should be warned that Christianity does not hold a monopoly on false friends. Going to church does not make one a Christian, any more than going to the cinema makes one a film director. The same is true of any faith, *including Buddhism*. Reverend Master Jiyu-Kennett was clear on this point and warned against putting absolute faith in any master:

> It is extraordinarily difficult to explain how the master–discipleship relationship works but, as a rule of thumb, it must be understood that if

the master requires the disciple to give up his will and/or surrender his body to him, then he is no master and there is no spiritual relationship.[8]

The Buddha himself warned against unconditionally accepting everything he said simply because he said it. His advice was to try out his teachings first, rather than to slavishly follow his words of wisdom regardless of any benefit that may or may not accrue. *Roshi* worship, the misguided belief that one's Zen teacher is an authority on every subject, and the disappointment and disillusionment that follows when one recognizes that even Zen masters can be appallingly ignorant, has no place in Zen. Roshi Philip Kapleau could not have been more frank when he was asked, "'Is an enlightened person enlightened about everything?" Roshi Kapleau replied, "To imagine that enlightenment brings an instant understanding of history, economics, politics, or anything like that is foolish. In Japan I met many spiritually developed people whose opinions on such subjects I would not have trusted.'"[9] Enlightenment is no more capable of making one an authority on all subjects than restoring a receding hairline or reducing a maturing waistline.

Dokusan

Traditionally found in all Zen schools, *dokusan* today functions mostly in the Rinzai Zen school. This is the formal, private meeting between master and pupil. Here, the pupil is given the chance to express any concerns he may have over his meditation techniques. For his part, the master has the opportunity to assess the progress of his pupil in regard to meditation in general, and koan practice in particular. It is in this personal encounter that the master will determine whether the pupil is ready to progress to the next koan.

Kyosaku

Again peculiar to (not all forms of) Rinzai Zen, this "encouragement stick" is not a punitive device for inflicting pain and introducing humiliation and embarrassment before one's colleagues. Sometimes found up to a metre long, its purpose is to return the mind wandering in *zazen* to its focus. What is more well known in the West as a "butterfly mind", is referred to in Zen as a "monkey mind", an apt description for the mind that jumps around from one place to another much like the antics of our forest cousins. Accordingly, a monitor will patrol the *zendo*, periodically giving a sharp thwack to any meditator who appears to be day-dreaming or, worse, snoozing. Not all masters make free use of the *kyosaku*, and some have openly criticized it:

> I was never comfortable with what I saw as the extreme, samurai-like use of the kyosaku. It seemed to go against the very heart of practice – namely that you are training because you want to liberate all sentient beings. To me, it felt contradictory to strike people with a stick to encourage them to do what they are already doing, had vowed to do, wanted to do and were striving mightily to do. Moreover, if you had to be hit in order to do the work, wouldn't you become dependent upon someone pushing you and exhorting you to do what should be your own responsibility.[10]

Rinzai Zen not only eschews all the established ceremonies and rituals of religion but also conventional intellectualism. However, I have said earlier that Rinzai and Western Ch'an do not reject understanding the purpose and function of meditation in general and koan practice in particular. Zen masters try to break down all the traditional, conventional ways of thinking. This may be done in ways that seem odd to a Westerner. As we have seen already, a visitor to a Zen monastery, for example, may be kept waiting outside all day and all night. Such actions are designed to apply a blow to the mind, just as Rinzai Zen teachers may also apply one to the body of a pupil from time to time. In Japan, this kind of teaching was thought to be thoroughly refreshing; conventional religions supported the idea that sense is acquired through the laws of thought and the result of reasoning and logic, but since Buddha-nature is beyond this, Zen tries to go beyond sense too, to non-logical sense. In Zen Buddhism, the individual is taken to the limits of thought, but not through dogmas, codes of ethics, or other such formulae. All the objects of the senses and emotions, philosophies and *isms* of any sort are overthrown and cast aside, so that the individual cannot be trapped in set patterns or be a slave to the kind of knowledge which is knowledge *about*, factual knowledge. Thoughts must be pushed, as it were, to the borders of a precipice and then beyond. Conventional thought and adherence to orthodox concepts only serve to prevent the intuitive understanding of the Buddha-nature within.

The master–pupil relationship is an important one in Zen, but since its abiding teaching is that mankind lacks only awakening, it is the pupil who is often expected to provide the answers to the problem. Accordingly, the Zen master is not seen as some didactic teacher whose every word must be obeyed without question. He is necessary because the truth about life cannot adequately be conveyed by the written word, but he is not the font of all knowledge, simply a spiritual guide that points the way to a truth that can only be realized by the pupil. Indeed, almost thirteen hundred years ago, the founder of the so-called Sudden school of Zen in China, Hui-neng, raised the question of whether a teacher *is* necessary for every student:

> The complete discourses of all Buddhas of past, present, and future are inherent in the essence of the human being. If you cannot realize this on your own, you need the guidance of a teacher to see it. As for those who do realize on their own, they do not need to seek elsewhere. If you insist that a teacher is necessary to attain liberation, you are wrong. Why? Because there is a teacher within your own mind who enlightens you spontaneously!

A lay Buddhist, recently locked into a seemingly imponderable problem, reluctantly concluded after much deliberation that the realization of its solution was beyond his competence. He therefore determined to visit his abbot, a drive that took many hours. Although he was expected, the abbot seemed in no great hurry to see his pupil and could be seen occupying himself with seemingly unimportant tasks for what seemed an eternity, while the pupil waited in anguish. At long last, he was summoned to the abbot, who listened patiently to the "insurmountable" problem. Having poured out his heart, the pupil waited expectantly for the words of wisdom that would ease his pain. He was prepared for a detailed analysis of the problem and its attendant solution, but as soon as he finished speaking was dumbfounded to find the abbot simply indicating the pupil's bench (a "bench" is what Soto Zen Buddhists call their meditation stool), and the abbot walked away. A thunderstruck pupil was left trying to cope with a flood of emotion, before reconciling himself to the fact that there was nothing he could do but heed the advice given, such as it was. The answer to his "insurmountable" problem came to him instantly!

10 Holding the Mind

For a hesitant beginner, whose mind is a mass of questions, to respond unquestioningly to the command "Sit and you will understand!" requires too demanding a leap of faith in his True-nature. Like an elephant which, it is said, will not walk over an unknown surface until it has first tested it to make sure it will bear its weight, the Zen newcomer needs to feel his way slowly, first satisfying his intellect that he is travelling in the right direction and then gaining the faith and confidence to go eventually he "knows not where by a road he knows not of".[1]

Some time ago, a university student kept an appointment with his dissertation supervisor who wished to ascertain his progress. The student proudly explained that for many months now he had been giving his work every consideration. He was able to speak articulately on his research, answering with authority each and every question put to him. He gave a detailed analysis of his wide reading, and was even able to elucidate over how, in the future, it was not inconceivable that he might be able to modify the views of positions long accepted as established in scholastic circles. He next described his conversations with similarly minded scholars, spoke with enthusiasm about the field trips that he had undertaken, and sat back in the chair smiling confidently, awaiting the unstinted praise he felt sure would come.

After what seemed an eternity, the supervisor finally spoke, "So where is the written work that you promised to give me today?" Starting to feel slightly embarrassed, but resisting the temptation to suggest to the professor that he must be patient, the student reminded his tutor that though, as yet, he had committed nothing to writing, the consideration that he had afforded his work was considerable. After another interminably long silence, the supervisor finally gave his assessment of the student's progress, "There comes a time when one must stop talking about it, stop wondering about it, stop pondering over it, and get down to *doing* it."

As we learned from the Ten Ox-herding Pictures, there comes a time when we must stop wondering about it, stop thinking about it, stop reading about it, and actually start *doing* it . . . "it" being Zen meditative practice. Before we start doing it, however, it is not unreasonable to ponder over how we might change as a result of *doing it*. Putting it crudely, (better, "egotistically") the question that could well be to the front of our minds is, "But what's in it for me?" As a note of caution, Wes Borden, Professor of Chemistry at the University of Washington, reminds us of the adage, "Be careful what you wish for, because you may get it."[2]

To suggest that meditative practice should be an easy task for the newcomer is foolish in the extreme: "I'm always having to rein in my thoughts, and when I meditate I feel tense from having to control my mind. I'm not at ease, and I can't concentrate very well"[3] is a commonly expressed concern. With the best will in the world, the meditator has to contend with an attention-seeking ego, filled with self-importance, false-pride and the like which demands attention through constant chatter, like the multifarious inhabitants of a tropical forest. With this attitude, and with the ego the centre of attention, practice can be extremely challenging, as one exasperated meditator recently admitted on his first retreat:[4]

> Why am I here, why am I putting myself through this. I'm cold and hungry and tired. My back aches . . . why do I have to sit and talk to this person. Why should I sit still and meditate. I don't want to know who they bloody are. I don't want to know who I am. I just want to go home to my wife and my nice warm bed.

However, when we still the mind and the chattering ceases, although the ego doesn't go away, it is no longer attention-seeking, it is simply there, like a sleeping child, and we come face to face with reality, for in the words of Reverend Master Daishin Morgan:

> If one learns how to be still, then that which underlies the sense of ego, the sense of "me", the sense of self-importance and so on is simply there, it doesn't demand acknowledgement, it is simply there of itself . . . so when

we turn to look we can begin to see it, and this is what we call Buddha-nature.

If there is one thing that the ego loves to be told, it is that there is going to be talk of the self. Even better is the promise that, through meditation, we are going to learn more about ourself, our true self that is. Clearly, this is something to be relished, since we will now be presented with the opportunity to come face-to-face with the many qualities that we undoubtedly have, something that modesty normally forbids. Hopefully, before too long, we may even be able to rejoice in the crowning glory of *satori*, then the world *will* be our oyster.

After we sit down in meditation and we clear the mind, the chattering ceases. What happens next? We do not need to be a professor of chemistry to envisage a rather large glass beaker filled with water. The water appears perfectly still (like our mind) but before too long a very small bubble of air forms on the bottom of the beaker. It then breaks contact with the glass and wends its way slowly and tortuously to the surface. This best describes how a thought comes to mind in meditation when the mind is supposedly stilled. It also comes as something of a shock to the ego to recognize that the thought that has surfaced does not represent something of which we are necessarily proud. Indeed, this thought may well reflect an aspect of our personality of which we are deeply ashamed, which is why it has been suppressed, lurking at the bottom of the glass so to speak. Far from being presented with recognition of our outstanding qualities, far too numerous to list here, in meditation we are *confronted* with a weakness that we earnestly seek to deny, but one that is nevertheless an integral part of our unique and peculiar character. One objection to this description of what happens in meditative practice could well be, "But doesn't enlightenment clear away imperfections and personality flaws?" When asked this exact same question, Roshi Philip Kapleau responded, "No, it shows them up!"[5]

Great Master Dogen outlined his *Rules for Meditation*, which should be effectuated in a quiet room:

> When meditating, do not wear tight clothing. Rest the left hand in the palm of the right hand with the thumbs touching lightly; sit upright, leaning neither to left nor right, backwards nor forwards. The ears must be in line with the shoulders and the nose in line with the navel; the tongue must be held lightly against the back of the top teeth with the lips and teeth closed. Keep the eyes open, breathe in quickly, settle the body comfortably and breathe out sharply. Sway the body left and right then

sit steadily, neither trying to think nor trying not to think; just sitting, with no deliberate thought, is the important aspect of serene reflection meditation.[6]

Admirable this may be, but the newcomer to meditation could well be forgiven for thinking, "If I only do this for two periods of some twenty or thirty minutes a day, how on earth does this influence the other twenty-three hours?" Zen Buddhism has an expression known as "working for oneself". In this mindset, one's workplace (no matter how oppressive) becomes the *zendo*, one's immediate task in hand (no matter how tiresome) becomes one's Zen practice. Bringing the mind of meditation out of the quiet room and into the noisy world, the "real world" of work and stress, is no easy task. Known as "working meditation", the method to achieve this transfer is ably summarized in five steps by Reverend Daizui MacPhillamy:[7]

1 Do one thing at a time.
2 Pay attention to what you are doing.
3 When your mind wanders to something else, bring it back.
4 Repeat step number three a few hundred thousand times.
5 But if your mind keeps wandering to the same thing over and over, stop for a minute; maybe it is trying to tell you something important.

I shall not insult the reader by analyzing each of these points in turn; we do not need reminding how desultory our mind (our "monkey mind" as Zen calls it) can be, a failing of which we are all too aware. Suffice it for me to quote the words of a visitor to a monastery (albeit of a different Buddhist tradition) who encountered this self-same attitude in the kitchen:

> When helping to prepare the one meal of the day for a community of around twenty people, the writer thought it might be a good opportunity to ask the novice nun, who was the only other helper in the kitchen, everything she wanted to know about Buddhism. However, the reply was, *I cannot talk now as I must concentrate on the task in hand.* Every action required mindfulness whether it was how carefully the vegetables were chopped or how the waste should be disposed of.[8]

Friends who come to my home and express an interest in milking my goats for the first time, always speak of a deep satisfaction in "being at one with myself", or "being close to the earth". The emotion they are voicing is their being mindful of what they are doing at the time, living in the moment (as do our pets and small children) rather than fretting about what they have to do next.

For what else is there but the pure act – the lifting of the hammer, the washing of the dish, the movement of the hands on the typewriter, the pulling of the weed? Everything else – thoughts of the past, fantasies about the future, judgments and evaluations concerning the work itself – what are these but shadows and ghosts flickering about in our minds, preventing us from entering fully into life itself?[9]

Perhaps working meditation can help us. The work pressures in twenty-first century society are considerable, often immoral. A close acquaintance recently was successfully interviewed by a line-manager for a position in a call centre. On her first day, towards noon, she enquired over the time and duration of the lunch break. The supervisor kindly explained that, of course, every employee was entitled to a lunch break and she could leave her workstation for a period of up to an hour. Smiling gently, he next put his arm around her shoulder and whispered, "But have a look around you, Mary. Do you see any of the other girls taking a lunch break? Why not grab a sandwich and get on with the work for which you are being paid." The new appointee was diabetic.

In the face of a constant stream of advice from the line-manager, from the government, indeed, from scriptures various to "do as you are told", it is refreshing to come across a religion that says the opposite. Although the Buddha proposed a panacea for suffering, he never once held himself up as a figure in authority. As surely as readers should not accept as gospel every thought and opinion I have expressed in this book (indeed, they would be foolhardy to do so) time and again the Buddha told his followers *not* to accept his advice simply because it was the word of Buddha, even if his advice did make good sense. Rather, he told them to try it and see, see whether their quality of life had improved by following Buddhist practice.

A while ago, I was in conversation with a scholar in another field; he asked me to summarize my attitude to life in a sentence. After giving the request careful consideration, I said that I thought I could best be described as a student of life, someone who, no matter how imperfectly, earnestly seeks to determine the true meaning of life. He then asked me what I was researching at the time. I explained that I was writing a book on Zen Buddhism; I added that this should help me in my quest. After mulling over my response for some time, he retorted that if I wrote a book on Zen, this would help me understand Zen; it would be of no use whatever in helping me to understand life. It is my sincere wish that readers of this modest book will disagree.

Notes

Introduction

1 H. Benoit, *The Light of Zen in the West*, incorporating *The Supreme Doctrine* and *The Realization of the Self*. Translated from the French by Graham Rooth (Brighton and Portland: Sussex Academic Press, 2004. *The Supreme Doctrine* was originally published in two volumes in French in 1951 and 1952), p. 150.

2 The autumn of 2004 saw BBC1 television run a series of eight programmes entitled *Should I worry about?* Each week viewers were presented with what was, supposedly, a different cause for concern.

3 H. Dumoulin, *Zen Buddhism in the 20th Century* (New York: Weatherhill, 1992), p. 88.

4 D. Goleman, *Emotional Intelligence: Why it can matter more than IQ* (London: Bloomsbury, 1996).

5 Goleman, *ibid.,* p. 311, note 4, acknowledges his debt to 'Paul Ekman's key essay, "An Argument for Basic Emotions", *Cognition and Emotion*, 6, 1992, pp. 169–200'.

6 Shen-yen, *Faith in Mind: A Guide to Ch'an Practice* (New York: Dharma Drum Publications, 1989), p. 73.

7 *Soto Zen Buddhism*, video produced by Wessex Consortium (1990).

8 A point made by Desmond Morris when working on his research fellowship in 1977 at Oxford University. His research was entitled *Manwatching*.

9 Benoit, *The Light of Zen in the West*, p. 12. However, Heinrich Dumoulin, *A History of Zen Buddhism* (London: Faber and Faber, 1963), p. 281, warns that psychology cannot speak the last word on Zen.

10 Dr Juliette Boutonnier, *L'Angoisse* (Paris: Presses Universitaire de France), cited in Benoit, p. xi.

11 C. Humphreys, in D. T. Suzuki, *An Introduction to Zen Buddhism* (London: Rider, 1991. First published Kyoto: The Eastern Buddhist Society, 1934. Revised edn with a foreword by C. G. Jung, London, 1960), p. 6.

12 *Ibid.*, p. 38.

1 The Ox-herding Pictures

1   E. Herrigel, *Zen in the Art of Archery* (London: Routledge and Kegan Paul, 1982. First published 1953), p. 19.
2   D. T. Suzuki, in E. Herrigel, *Zen in the Art of Archery* (London: Routledge and Kegan Paul, 1982. First published 1953), p. 7.
3   I am indebted to Hubert Benoit for this analogy.

2 Zen Roots

1   D. T. Suzuki, *An Introduction to Zen Buddhism* (London: Rider, 1991. First published Kyoto: The Eastern Buddhist Society, 1934), p. 41.
2   S. Ohasama and A. Faust, *Zen: der lebendige Buddhismus in Japan* (Gotha, 1925), p. ix.
3   See M. D. Fowler, "Excavated Figurines: A Case for Identifying a Site as Sacred?" in *Zeitschrift fur die alttestamentliche Wissenschaft*, Band 97, Heft 3 (Berlin: De Gruyter, 1985), pp. 333–44.
4   R. T. H. Griffith, *The Hymns of the Rg Veda* (Delhi: Motilal Banarsidass, 1991 reprint of new revised 1973 edn), p. 130.
5   A. L. Basham, *The Wonder that was India* (London: Sidgwick and Jackson, 1982 reprint of third revised 1967 edn), p.235.
6   Sangharakshita, *The Eternal Legacy* (London: Tharpa 1985), p. 16, notes that the *canonical* Jataka stories of the previous lives of the Buddha depict him as a wise man of old. It is only the much later *non-canonical* stories of the Theravada Jataka Book which relate the Buddha's lives as an animal. See R. Chalmers, W. H. D. Rouse, *Jataka* (three vols) (Oxford: The Pali Text Society, 1995. First published by Cambridge University Press, 1895).
7   Sangharakshita, *The Eternal Legacy*, p. 2, warns that, strictly speaking, Pali is not the name of a language at all: 'The word means literally, "a line, a row [of letters]" and thus, by extension of its meaning, "the [canonical] text". Early Western students of Theravada literature, finding in the commentaries expressions such as *palinayena*, "according to the [canonical] text", took the word for the name of the *language*, of the texts and, through their writings, gave currency to this misunderstanding.'
8   R. F. Gombrich,"'Dating the Buddha: A Red Herring Revealed", in H. Bechert (ed.), *The Dating of the Historical Buddha*, Part 2 (Gottingen 1992), pp. 237–59. Cf. R. F. Gombrich, *How Buddhism Began: The Conditioned Genesis of the Early Teachings* (London: Athlone 1996), p. 76, note 11.
9   M. Pye, *The Buddha* (London: Duckworth 1979), p. 11.
10 M. Carrithers, *The Buddha* (Oxford: Oxford University Press, 1983), p. 13.
11 Book I: 34. Text in E. B. Cowell (trans),*The Buddha Carita or the Life of the Buddha* (New Delhi: Cosmo 1977). First published 1894, first Indian print 1977. Unless stated otherwise, all references to the *Buddhacarita* are from Cowell.
12 Although it is only right that the reader's attention throughout this work should be drawn to the Indian background of Buddhism, this in no way is

to suggest that Buddhism is no more than a form of Hinduism, a point well made by Professor Gombrich; see *How Buddhism Began*, especially pp. 14–15.

13 *The Buddha*, p. 26.

14 *The Buddha*, p. 31.

15 E. Conze (trans.), *Buddhist Scriptures* (London: Penguin 1959), p. 50.

16 W. Rahula, *What the Buddha Taught* (New York: Grove, 1996 reprint of 2nd edition 1974. First published 1959), p.41.

17 E. Conze, *Buddhist Scriptures*, p. 51.

18 A. Powell, *Living Buddhism* (London: British Museum 1989), p. 14.

19 E. Conze, *Buddhist Scriptures*, p. 57.

20 E. Conze, *Buddhist Scriptures*, p. 53.

21 M. Carrithers, *The Buddha*, p. 98.

3 Doctrines Germane to Zen

1 J. M. Koller, *The Indian Way* (London: Macmillan, 1982), p.137.

2 See W. Rahula, *What the Buddha Taught* (Oxford: Oneworld, 1998 reprint of 1st 1959 edn), p. 2, note 1, for definition of *sangha*.

3 See reverend Master Jiyu-Kennett, "Perfect Faith" in *An Introduction to the Tradition of Serene Reflection Meditation* (Mount Shasta, CA: Shasta Abbey Press, 1998. First published 1986), pp. 37 and 40.

4 T. R. V. Murti, *The Central Philosophy of Buddhism; A Study of the Madhyamika System* (London: Unwin, 1987. First published 1955), p. 19.

5 *What the Buddha Taught*, p. 17.

6 The observation is not mine but Sangharakshita's.

7 M. Pye, *The Buddha* (London: Duckworth,1979), p.48.

8 E. Conze, *Buddhism: its essence and development* (New Delhi: Munshiram Manoharial, 2001. First published by Bruno Cassirer, Oxford, 1951), pp. 18–19.

9 Conze, *ibid.*, p.107.

10 J. M. Koller, *The Indian Way*, p.158.

11 E. Conze, *Buddhism: its essence and development*, p. 29.

12 *Buddhism: A Very Short Introduction* (Oxford: Oxford University Press, 1996), p. 53. The problem that the Buddhist has with desire is discussed admirably by Michael Carrithers in *The Buddha*, p. 77.

13 E. Conze, *Buddhist Scriptures* (London: Penguin, 1959), p.72.

4 Zen and the Mahayana Sutras

1 H. Dumoulin, *A History of Zen Buddhism* (London: Faber and Faber, 1963), p. 269.

2 See especially P. Harrison, "Searching for the Origins of the Mahayana: What are we looking for?" in *The Eastern Buddhist* vol. V (Kyoto, 1995), pp. 48–69.

3 D. T. Suzuki, *An Introduction to Zen Buddhism* (London: Rider, 1992. First published Kyoto: The Eastern Buddhist Society, 1934), p. 38.

4 *The Zen Monastic Experience: Buddhist Practice in Contemporary Korea* (Princeton University Press, 1992).

5 *The Zen Doctrine of No Mind* (London: Rider, 1991. First published 1949), p. 14.

6 M. Goodson, "Introduction to Zen Practice: Some Points to Remember", *The Middle Way*, vol.71, no. 4 (London: The Buddhist Society, February 1997), p. 212.

7 R. E. Buswell, Jr., *The Zen Monastic Experience*, p. 17.

8 *Ibid.*, p. 218.

9 J. D. Fowler, *Hinduism: beliefs and practices* (Brighton and Portland: Sussex Academic Press, 1997), p. 86.

10 S. Schuhmacher, G. Woerner (eds), *The Rider Encyclopedia of Eastern Philosophy and Religion* (London: Rider, 1986).

11 Dumoulin, *Zen Buddhism. A History. Vol. 1, India and China* (London and New York: Macmillan, 1988), p. 21.

5   Buddhism reaches China

1 H. Maspero, *Taoism and Chinese Religion*. Originally published as *Le Taoisme et les religions chinoises*, 1971. Translated from the French by F. A. Kierman, Jr. (Amhurst: The University of Massachusetts Press, 1981), p. 252.

2 Maspero, *Taoism and Chinese Religion*, p. 38.

3 *Ibid.*, p. 39.

4 *Ibid.*, p. 258.

5 T. Fletcher and D. Scott, *Way of Zen* (London: Vega, 2001), p. 37.

6 I. Robinet (P. Brooks trans.), *Taoism. Growth of a Religion* (Stanford, CA: Stanford University Press, 1997), p.188.

7 Of the three credible texts from an early period that help to throw possible light on the historicity of Bodhidharma, the two main sources are in disagreement concerning the place where Bodhidharma first set foot on Chinese soil. See H. Dumoulin, *Zen Buddhism. A History. Volume 1, India and China* (London, New York: Macmillan, 1988), p. 90.

8 *Zen Buddhism: A History. Volume 1, India and China*, p. 89.

9 See Sangharakshita, *The Essence of Zen* (Glasgow: Windhorse, 1992), p. 25.

10 Dumoulin, *Zen Buddhism. A History. Volume 1, India and China*, p. 85.

11 Venerable Myoko-ni, "Zen – Tradition and History", in *The Middle Way*, vol. 73, no.1 (London: The Buddhist Society, May 1998), p.14.

12 Ruth Fuller Sasaki, in Yanagida Seizan, *Chugoku zenshushi* (History of the Zen School in China), Volume 3 of *Zen no rekishi* (History of Zen), edited by D. T. Suzuki and K. Nishitani (Tokyo, 1974), p. 8 following.

13 Dumoulin, *Zen Buddhism. A History. Volume 1, India and China*, p. 86.

14 Katsuki Sekida (translated with commentaries) *Two Zen Classics:*

Mumonkan and Hekiganroku, edited by A. V. Grimstone (New York: Weatherhill, 1977), Case 41, Bodhidharma's Mind Pacifying.

15 K. Ch'en, *Buddhism in China. A Historical Survey* (Princeton University Press, 1974), p. 353.

16 Yu-lan, Fung, *A History of Chinese Philosophy Volume 2,* (Derk Bodde trans.) (Princeton University Press, 1952), p. 388.

17 *Ibid.*

18 K. Ch'en, *Buddhism in China,* p. 354.

19 R. E. Buswell, Jr., *The Zen Monastic Experience: Buddhist Practice in Contemporary Korea* (Princeton University Press, 1992), p. 220.

20 A concise biography of Hui-neng is found in Dumoulin, *Zen Buddhism. A History. Volume I, India and China,* pp. 129–37.

21 Dumoulin, *A History of Zen Buddhism* (London: Faber and Faber, 1963), p. 104.

22 Robinet, *Taoism. Growth of a Religion,* p. 187.

23 Dumoulin, *Zen Buddhism. A History. Vol 1, India and China,* p. 179.

24 Fletcher and Scott, *Way of Zen,* p. 58.

25 D. Wile, *Art of the Bedchamber. The Chinese Sexual Yoga Classics including Women's Solo Meditation Texts* (New York: State University of New York Press, hereafter SUNY, 1992), p. 191.

26 R. E. Allinson, "An Overview of the Chinese Mind", in R. E. Allinson (ed.) *Understanding the Chinese Mind: The Philosophical Roots* (Oxford: Oxford University Press, 1989), p. 15. See also note 6, p. 25.

27 *Ching-te ch'uan-teng-lu,* Vol. VI.

28 *Ibid.*

29 Katsuki Sekida, *Two Zen Classics.* Case 14. Nansen Cuts the Cat in Two.

30 *Ibid.,* Case 28. Ryutan blows out the Candle.

31 I am indebted to Rupert Gethin for this stark observation. See *The Foundations of Buddhism* (Oxford: Oxford University Press, 1998).

32 R. E. Buswell, Jr., *The Zen Monastic Experience,* p. 4.

33 D. T. Suzuki, *The Training of the Zen Buddhist Monk* (Boston: Charles Tuttle, 1994. First published Kyoto: The Eastern Buddhist Society, 1934), p. xi.

34 T. Cleary, *The Five Houses of Zen* (Boston: Shambala, 1997), pp. vii–xvii.

35 See especially chapters 7 and 9.

36 Katsuki Sekida, *Two Zen Classics* (New York: Weatherhill, 1977).

37 T. Cleary (trans.), *Book of Serenity* (New York: Lindisfarne, 1990).

38 H. Dumoulin, *A History of Zen Buddhism,* p. 195.

6 The Transition from China to Japan

1 A point well made by E. Herrigel, *Zen in the Art of Archery* (London: Routledge and Kegan Paul, 1982. First published 1953).

2 Translator A. W. Watts, *The Way of Zen* (Harmondsworth, Middlesex: Penguin, 1957), pp. 204–8.

3 *Ibid.*

4 *Ibid.*

5 Basho, *Haiku* (translator Lucien Stryk, London: Penguin 1995), pp. 4, 9, 18, 31 and 42, respectively.

6 H. Dumoulin, *Zen Buddhism: A History Vol. 2 Japan* (London: Macmillan, 1990), p. 14.

7 H. Dumoulin, *A History of Zen Buddhism* (London: Faber and Faber, 1963), p. 233.

8 *Ibid.*, p. 265.

9 M. Batchelor, *The Way of Zen* (London: Thorsons, 2001), p. 43.

10 *Ibid.*, p. 44.

11 *Ibid.*

7 Meditation

1 S. Graef, "Seeing the Ox: A Second Look", in *Zen Teaching, Zen Practice* edited by Kenneth Kraft (New York: Weatherhill, 2000), p.113.

2 P. Kapleau, in Thich Nhat Hanh, *Zen Keys* (London: Doubleday, 1995. First English edn New York: Anchor: Doubleday, 1974), p.8.

3 H. Dumoulin, *Zen Buddhism. A History. Vol. 1, India and China* (New York and London: Macmillan, 1988), p. xvii.

4 D. T. Suzuki, *The Training of the Zen Buddhist Monk* (Boston: Charles Tuttle, 1994 reprint of the 1934 edn, Kyoto: The Eastern Buddhist Society), p. x.

5 Alan Watts, *The Way of Zen* (London: Arkana, 1990, reprint of 1957 edn), p. 105.

6 J. D. Fowler "Buddhism", in J. D. Fowler *et al. World Religions: An Introduction for Students* (Brighton and Portland: Sussex Academic Press, second edn 1999. First edn 1997), p. 270.

7 W. Rahula, *What the Buddha Taught* (Oxford: Oneworld, 1998 reprint of first 1959 edn), p. 67 especially note 2. The chapter on "Meditation or Mental Culture", pages 67–75, remains one of the best.

8 Reverend Kinrei Bassis, "Not Necessary, But Useful", *The Journal of Shasta Abbey* (Mount Shasta, CA: Shasta Abbey Press.), vol. xv, no. 4, p.2.

9 I am indebted to Rohit Mehta for this analogy. See *The Call of the Upanisads* (Delhi: Motilal Banarsidass, 1990. First published 1970).

10 D. T. Suzuki, *An Introduction to Zen Buddhism* (London: Rider, 1991. First published, Kyoto: The Eastern Buddhist Society, 1934.) p. 41.

11 As in the last chapter of this book entitled "Holding the Mind". See, among many others, H. Dumoulin, *A History of Zen Buddhism* (London: Faber and Faber, 1963. first published 1959), p. 161 for Dogen's description of sitting meditation, also J. Clark, "Introduction to Zen Practice", *The Middle Way*, vol. 71, no. 3 (November 1996), p. 158. See also J. Clark, "Everyday Practice", *The Middle Way*, vol. 73, no. 1(May 1998), pp. 21–2, and "Everyday Practice, part three", *The Middle Way*, vol. 73, no. 3 (November 1998), pp. 134–6, by the same author.

12 J. Crook "Awareness in Everyday Life", in *Western Ch'an Forum* (Lancs: The Western Ch'an Fellowship, Autumn 1995), pp. 14–15.

13 http://www.throssel.org.uk/srm.htms

14 K. Jones, *The Social Face of Buddhism: An Approach to Political and Social Activism* (London: Wisdom, 1989), p. 45.

15 Yasutani Roshi, cited in K. Kraft, *Zen Teaching, Zen Practice* (New York: Weatherhill, 2000), p. 14.

16 H. Dumoulin, *A History of Zen Buddhism* (London: Faber and Faber, 1963), p. 290. Several fascinating examples of the *satori* experience are given on pp. 273–5.

17 Reprinted in *An Introduction to the Tradition of Serene Reflection Meditation* (Mount Shasta, CA: Shasta Abbey Press, 1997. First edn 1986), pp. 32–6.

18 *Serene Reflection Meditation Pamphlet* (no date), p. 2.

19 Reverend Master Jiyu-Kennett, *An Introduction to the Tradition of Serene reflection Meditation* (Mount Shasta, CA: Shasta Abbey Press, 1997), p. 39. See also, H. Benoit, *The Light of Zen in the West*, translated from the French by Graham Rooth (Brighton and Portland: Sussex Academic Press, 2004), p. 154. This work incorporates *The Supreme Doctrine* and *The Realization of the Self*. *The Supreme Doctrine* was originally published as two separate volumes in French in 1951 and 1952.

20 Venerable Myoko-ni, "Zen – Tradition and History", in *The Middle* Way, vol. 73, no. 1, May 1998), p. 17.

21 H. Benoit, *The Supreme Doctrine,* in *The Light of Zen in the West*, Graham Rooth (trans.) (Brighton and Portland: Sussex Academic Press, 2004), p. 31.

22 P. Yampolsky (trans.), *The Zen Master Hakuin* (New York, 1971), p. 170.

23 Brian Gay, a lay minister of the Order of Buddhist Contemplatives in conversation with the author.

8 Koan Practice

1 Cited in H. Benoit, *The Supreme Doctrine,* in *The Light of Zen in the West* (G. Rooth translator, Brighton and Portland: Sussex Academic Press, 2004), p. 155.

2 R. E. Allinson, *Chang-Tzu for Spiritual Transformation* (New York: SUNY, 1989), p. 9.

3 Isshu Miura and Ruth Fuller Sasaki, *The Zen Koan: Its History and Use in Rinzai Zen* (New York: Harcourt, Brace and World, 1965), pp. xi–xii.

4 See Michael Lafargue, *Tao and Method. A Reasoned Approach to the Tao Te Ching* (Albany, New York: SUNY, 1994), p. 212 for a full and interesting discussion of the meaning of *wu*.

5 J. Crook, "The Place of Ch'an in Modern Europe", *Chung-Hwa Buddhist Journal*, vol. 13.2 (Taipei, 2000), p. 551.

6 I am indebted to W. Owen Cole for this observation.

7 Chung-Yin Cheng, "Chinese Metaphysics as Non-Metaphysics: Confucian

and Taoist Insights into the Nature of Reality", in R. E. Allinson (ed.), *Understanding the Chinese Mind: The Philosophical Roots* (Oxford: Oxford University Press, 1989), p. 192.

8 Wing-tsit Chan (translator and compiler), *A Source Book in Chinese Philosophy* (Princeton University Press and London: Oxford University Press, 1963), p. 791.

9 C. Luk, *The Secrets of Chinese Meditation* (London: Rider, 1964), p. 44.

10 An excellent discussion of Being and Non-Being is to be found in Toshihiko Izutsu, *Sufism and Taoism* (Berkeley: University of California Press, 1984), Chapter VII "The Way", pp. 375–97. The complexity of the definition of *wu* is attested in Alan K. L. Chan, "A Tale of Two Commentaries" in Livia Kohn and Michael LaFargue (eds), *Lao-tzu and the* Tao-te-ching (Albany, New York: SUNY, 1998), p.103. The interested reader is also referred to Isabelle Robinet, "The Diverse Interpretations of the Laozi", in Mark Csikszentmihalyi and Philip J. Ivanhoe (eds), *Religious and Philosophical Aspects of the Laozi* (Albany, New York: SUNY, 1999), pp. 138–43. See also, R. P. Peerenboom, "Cosmogany, The Taoist way", in *The Journal of Chinese Philosophy* Vol. 17 (1990), pp. 157–74, especially pp. 166–74.

11 H. Benoit, *The Supreme Doctrine*, p. 99.

12 W. Borden "Tall Branches, Tender Leaves", in K. Kraft (ed.), *Zen Teaching, Zen Practice* (New York: Weatherhill, 2000), pp. 38–40.

13 C. Luk, *The Secrets of Chinese Meditation* (London: Rider, 1964), p. 46.

14 A. V. Grimstone, in Katsuki Sekida (trans.) *Two Zen Classics: Mumonkan and Hekiganroku* (New York: Weatherhill, 1996. First published 1977), p. 15.

15 T. Cleary, *Kensho. The Heart of Zen* (London: Shambhala, 1997), p. xi.

16 H. Dumoulin, *Zen Buddhism in the 20th Century* (New York: Weatherhill, 1992), p. 122.

9 The Master–Pupil Relationship

1 A point made long ago by Candrakirti (flourished between 600 and 650 CE).

2 S. W. Smithers, "Spiritual Guide", in *ER,* vol. 14, p. 34.

3 M. Waida, "Authority", in *ER,* vol. 2, p. 3.

4 D. T. Suzuki, "An Interpretation of Zen Experience," in *The Japanese Mind: Essentials of Japanese Philosophy and Culture*, ed. Charles A. Moore, (Honolulu: University of Hawaii Press, 1967), p. 123.

5 T. Cleary, *Kensho. The Heart of Zen* (London: Shambala, 1997), p. xi.

6 Great Master Dogen, "Shushogi. What is Truly Meant by Training and Enlightenment", reprinted in *An Introduction to the Tradition of Serene Reflection Meditation* (Mount Shasta, CA: Shasta Abbey Press, 1997), p. 13.

7 "Merton the Prophet", in Paul Wilks (ed.), *Merton By Those Who Knew Him Best* (San Francisco: Harper and Row, 1984), p. 43.

8 *An Introduction to the Tradition of Serene Reflection Meditation* (Mount Shasta, CA: Shasta Abbey Press, 1998. First published 1986), p. 38.

9 Cited in W. Borden, "Tall Branches, Tender Leaves", in K. Kraft (ed.), *Zen Teaching, Zen Practice* (New York: Weatherhill, 2000), p. 31.

10 S. Graef, "Seeing the Ox: A Second Look", in K. Kraft (ed.), *Zen Teaching, Zen Practice* (New York: Weatherhill, 2000), p. 115.

10 Holding the Mind

1 P. Kapleau, *Zen* (London: Rider, 1980), p. 3.

2 "Tall Branches, Tender Leaves", in K. Kraft (ed.), *Zen Teaching, Zen Practice* (New York: Weatherhill, 2000), p. 43.

3 Ajahn Sucitto, "Confidence: Holding the Mind", in *The Middle Way*, vol. 79, no. 2 (August–October 2004), p. 67.

4 The various hindrances to establishing a regular meditation practice are addressed by Ajahn Sucitto, *ibid.*, pp. 67–73.

5 P. Kapleau, *Zen: Merging of East and West* (New York: Anchor Doubleday, 1989), p. 31.

6 Reprinted in *An Introduction to the Tradition of Serene Reflection Meditation* (Mount Shasta, CA: Shasta Abbey Press, 1997), pp. 17–19.

7 "Every-minute Meditation", *ibid.*, p. 20.

8 Y. S. Chindoo-Roy, *Aspects of Theravada Buddhism* (Unpublished BA dissertation submitted to the University of Wales, 1990), p. 49.

9 P. Kapleau, in Thich Nhat Hanh, *Zen Keys* (London: Doubleday, 1995. First English edn, New York: Anchor, 1974), p. 3.

Glossary

Abhidamma	Pali (Skt. *Abhidharma*): one of the "Three Baskets" of Buddhist scriptures containing discussion and commentary on the teaching of the Buddha; literally "higher knowledge".
ahimsa	the doctrine of non-violence in relation to all living things.
Amitabha	the mythical buddha of the Western Paradise. Conspicuous and much revered in the Jodo Shien Shu sect of Japanese Buddhism. It is held that by the saving grace of Amitabha *nirvana* can be realized.
anatta	Pali (Skt. *anatman*): the Buddhist doctrine of no-self.
anicca	Pali (Skt. *anitya*): the Buddhist doctrine of impermanence – that nothing ever *is* but is always in a state of *becoming*.
arahant	Pali (Skt. *arhat*): an enlightened person. This is the ideal of the Hinayana or Southern School of Buddhism.
Avalokitesvara	(Chin. Kuan-yin; Jap. Kwannon/Kanzen; Tibetan Chen-re-zig); the national bodhisattva (of compassion) of Tibet. Avalokitesvara is also the principal Bodhisattva in the Zen Buddhist tradition. Represented in male and female form, he embodies boundless compassion for all sentient beings.
bhikku (male)	a Buddhist monk.
bhikkuni (female)	a Buddhist nun.
Blue Cliff Record (Jap. *Hekiganroku*)	a collection of one hundred koans with commentaries. Compiled by Master Setcho Juken (980–1052).
Bodh Gaya	the place where the Buddha became enlightened and an important pilgrimage site.
bodhi	the Sanskrit term for enlightenment. The *bodhi* mind is an awakened mind.

bodhicitta	a Mahayana technical term meaning "the thought of enlightenment". It has a twofold application, encompassing the intention to become a Buddha for the sake of all sentient beings, and the effectuation of that intention.
Bodhidharma	an Indian meditation master, presumed to be the first Chinese patriarch and hence the founder of Ch'an Buddhism in China. Well known for his knowledge of the Lankavatara sutra, Bodhidharma is held to be the twenty-eighth Indian patriarch, having received the Dharma-seal from his master in India.
bodhisattva	a buddha to be; a major concept of Mahayana Buddhism where it is considered as the ideal. The term refers to one who vows to help all sentient beings to attain buddhahood, and who has delayed his own enlightenment to this end.
bodhi tree	the name given to the tree under which the Buddha was seated when he became enlightened.
brahma-vihara	four sublime states: see *metta, karuna, mudita, upekkha*.
buddha	one who is enlightened or awakened. Sakyamuni Buddha is the historical Buddha, literally the sage of the Sakya clan.
buddha-nature	the inherently pure nature within all things. It is a Mahayana notion that all beings possess this pure nature that is identical to that of the Buddhas, worldly or cosmic. This notion (that is absent from early, Hinayana Buddhism) becomes crystallized in Zen, where the teaching is that the Buddha-nature is not something that has to be *attained* but *realized*.
butsudan	a Japanese shrine.
Ch'an	Chinese for the Sanskrit word *dhyana* meaning "meditation", the name given to a school of Buddhism in China corresponding to, and being the foundation of, Japanese Zen.
Dalai Lama	spiritual head of Tibetan Buddhism. *Dalai* means "ocean" (of knowledge).
dhamma	Pali (Skt. *dharma*): a generic term with an enormous number of meanings, it is most generally used to represent the totality of the teaching of the Buddha; Truth.
Dhammapada	important and popular Buddhist scripture, the ethical content of which is both simple and edifying.
Dharmakaya	the "Truth body" of the Buddha; ultimate reality.
dhyana	see Ch'an.
Diamond Sutra	A much valued scripture in the Zen tradition; a section of the *Prajnaparamita Sutra*.

Dogen Kigen	one of Japanese Zen Buddhism's greatest figures. Dogen was the Zen master who returned from his travels in China with the tradition identified as Soto Zen in Japan.
dokusan	private, formal interviews with a *roshi*.
dukkha	Pali (Skt. *duhkha*): pain, suffering, dis-ease, disharmony. The first of the Four Noble Truths.
Eightfold Path	the last of the Four Noble truths advocates the following of the Noble Eightfold Path. This is a non-linear progression towards enlightenment.
Eisei	Myoan Esai *later* came to be regarded as the founder of Zen Buddhism in Japan.
Enlightenment	see *satori*.
han	a hanging wooden block, the striking of which marks the duration of *zazen*.
Hana Matsuri	Japanese Mahayana Buddhist festival.
Heart Sutra	a condensation of the *Prajnaparamita Sutra*, summarizing the most important teachings.
ino	one who leads the chanting.
jikido	the timekeeper throughout *zazen*.
jukai	Zen Buddhist ceremony wherein the student affirms his commitment to maintain the precepts.
junko	walking with the encouragement stick.
Higan	Japanese Mahayana Buddhist festivals held at the time of the equinoxes.
Hinayana	"Small vehicle" (to salvation), the pejorative term given by Mahayana Buddhists to the conservative Buddhist schools of thought. Modern scholars prefer the term "early Buddhism".
jakugo	the practice of summarizing an entire koan in one clue word; Joshu's *Mu* is a case in point.
Jatakas	stories relating the past lives of the Buddha.
jhana	Pali (Skt. *dhyana*): meditation.
jiriki	the path to enlightenment by "own effort".
Jodo-e	a Japanese Mahayana Buddhist festival.
Joya no Kane	a Japanese Mahayana Buddhist festival.
kamma	Pali (Skt. *karma*): action and the fruits of action.
karuna	compassion, one of the four *brahma-vihara*.
Reverend Master Jiyu-Kennett	until her death in 1996, the head and source of the Soto Zen Order in Britain. Founder of Throssel Hole Priory in Northumberland, England as well as Shasta Abbey on Mount Shasta, California.

kensho	often used synonymously with *satori*, another Zen technical term for "enlightenment", *kensho* more properly refers to an initial incomplete awakening.
khandas	Pali (Skt. *skandhas*) the five constituents which make up the self as we know it.
kinhin	*walking meditation.*
koan	peculiar to Zen, these *apparently* paradoxical riddles are held to be simple and clear statements made from the state of consciousness which they have helped to awaken.
Kusinara	the site of the Buddha's death and an important pilgrimage site.
kyosaku	the purpose of this "encouragement stick", sometimes found up to a metre long, is to return the mind wandering in *zazen* to its focus; peculiar to Rinzai Zen.
lama	a standard Tibetan translation of *guru*, a spiritual teacher, a title given to the religious leaders of the monastic traditions in Tibetan Buddhism.
Lumbini Garden	the place where the Buddha was born.
mahakaruna	great compassion, one of the two pillars of Mahayana Buddhism.
Mahaparinibbana-sutta	"Account of the Great Final *nibbana*", the death of the Buddha.
Mahayana	"Great vehicle" (to salvation), the name given to the more progressive strands which emerged from early, conservative Buddhism.
mandalas	geometric, symbolic designs used as aids in meditation.
mantra	symbolic sounds and words.
Mara	the Buddhist enemy of enlightenment.
metta	loving-kindness, one of the four *brahma-vihara*.
mondo	verbal interchange between Master and pupil in Rinzai Zen Buddhism.
Reverend Master Daishin Morgan	incumbent abbot at Throssel Hole Soto Zen Buddhist Priory, Northumberland, England. Order of Buddhist Contemplatives.
mu	see *wu*. Joshu's *mu* is often taken as the first koan in formal practice.
mudita	sympathetic joy, one of the four *brahma-vihara*.
mudra	symbolic hand positions.
Mumonkan	The Gateless gate. A collection of 48 koans compiled and annotated by Mumon Ekai, a thirteenth century Zen master.

Nahan-e	Japanese Mahayana Buddhist festival.
nembutsu	both a term meaning to meditate on a Buddha or invoke his name (in later usage it came to mean the recitation of Amida's name), and a generic term for those sects which seek to attain rebirth in the Pure Land by worshipping Amida Buddha.
nibbana	Pali (Skt. *nirvana*): enlightenment, total egolessness.
nirmanakaya	"transformation body", a manifestation of a buddha in earthly form.
Obon	a Japanese Mahayana Buddhist festival.
Order of Buddhist Contemplatives (O.B.C)	name given to the Soto Zen school in Britain.
pagoda	Japanese monument housing relics of the Buddha.
Pancha Sila	the Five Moral Precepts basic to most schools of Buddhism.
panna	Pali (Skt. *prajna*): wisdom which brings enlightenment.
parinibbana	Pali (Skt. *parinirvana*): the final extinction of the Buddha and the end of his rebirths.
Paramitas	the six perfections practised by *bodhisattvas*. They comprise wisdom, patience, generosity, meditative awareness, effort and precepts.
paticcasamuppada	the Buddhist doctrine of dependent origination.
prajna	see *panna*.
Prajnaparamita	literally "Perfection of Wisdom"; the most important literature for Mahayana Buddhism.
Precepts	The sixteen Buddhist precepts comprise the Three Treasures, the Three Pure Precepts and the Ten Grave Precepts.
puja	honour, respect, gratitude.
Rinzai Zen	school of Buddhism brought to Japan by Eisai Zenji (1141–1215). The Rinzai school continues the Lin-chi Ch'an tradition from China by combining meditative and koan practice.
Roshi	Zen master.
rupa	image of a buddha or *bodhisattva*.
Sakyas	(pronounced Shakya): tribe of people in northern India into which the Buddha was born.
Sakyamuni	(pronounced Shakyamuni): "Wise one from the Sakyas", the name given to the Buddha by many Mahayana Buddhists.

samadhi	concentration, one-pointed non-dualistic awareness, the advanced state of meditation.
samanna	Pali (Skt. *sramana*) one who rejected orthodox teachings and who searched for Truth independently.
samatha	meditation.
sambhogakaya	"glorious body" of a buddha.
samsara	the "aimless wandering"; the round of death and rebirth into which beings driven by craving are repeatedly born.
Sangha	the assembly of monks in Theravada Buddhism; the community of Buddhists in Mahayana Buddhism.
Sarnath Deer Park	the place where the Buddha taught his first sermon, and a place of pilgrimage.
satori	sudden, intuitive enlightenment in Rinzai Zen Buddhism; more gradual, after long periods of sitting meditation in Soto Zen.
sensei	authorized teacher.
Serene Reflection Meditation	the term used by the the Soto Zen school for *zazen*.
sesshin	a period of intensive *zazen* practised in a retreat usually of seven days duration.
Setsubon	a Japanese Mahayana Buddhist festival.
shikantaza	just sitting. *Zazen* bereft of breath control or koan practice.
Soto Zen	school of Buddhism brought to Japan by Dogen (1200–1253). It continues the Ts'ao-tung Ch'an tradition from China.
stupa	monument housing some relic(s) of the Buddha. See also *pagoda*.
Sukhavati	the paradisical realm of the Buddha Amida/Amitabha.
sunya	(pronounced *shunya*): empty.
sunyata	(pronounced *shunyata*): Emptiness, a major doctrine of Mahayana Buddhism that all things are empty of permanent essence.
sutta	Pali (Skt. *sutra*) one of "Three Baskets"; a general term for a scripture.
svabhava	own-being.
tanha	craving, the cause of suffering and the second of the Buddha's *Four Noble Truths*.
Tao	the non-manifest and manifest essence of the universe.
Tantrism	literally "loom"; the esoteric, mystical aspects of Buddhism.

tensho	head cook.
Theravada	"Way of the elders", the name given to the only surviving school of conservative Buddhism.
Three Jewels or *Three Refuges*	The Buddha, the *Dhamma* and the *Sangha*.
Throssel Hole	Soto Zen Priory in Northumberland, England.
Tipitaka	Pali (Skt. *Tripitaka*): "Three Baskets", the scriptures of Theravada Buddhism and some Mahayana.
upekkha	equanimity, one of the four *brahma-vihara*.
urna	the third eye of the Buddha.
usnisa	the projection on the top of the Buddha's head which signifies his spirituality and great mind.
Vesak/Wesak	festival which celebrates the Birth, Enlightenment and Death of the Buddha.
Vinaya	monastic rules, one of the "Three Baskets" which comprise orthodox Buddhist scriptures.
vipassana	insight meditiation.
wu	Chinese equivalent of the Japanese *satori*, enlightenment.
wu-wei	inaction; more properly "action in non-action", action that is not tainted by the three defilements of greed, anger and delusion. Traditional Chinese Taoist term for *nirvana*.
zazen	literally "sitting in meditation" and the name it is given in Japanese Zen Buddhism. *Zazen* is a technical term for the primary religious practice in Zen.
zafu	round, sitting cushions.
zendo	main meditation hall.

Further Reading

Whole libraries of books have been published on Zen; many have been written from a different perspective, each has its own particular place in the vast patchwork quilt known as Zen Buddhism. It would be quite wrong to describe this patchwork quilt as a jigsaw puzzle. This implies that once all the pieces in the jigsaw have been fitted together, a complete picture (and hence understanding) of Zen will evolve. But this is not the way of Zen. Zen is not meant to be understood, but experienced, and no amount of reading can ever provide this experience, no matter how skilled the authors. As surely as writers may approach their works on Zen from different angles, so, too, each reader may have a particular approach to Zen that is meaningful to them, that they wish to pursue. I have tried to address the needs of a variety of readers below.

For the reader who simply (but crucially) wants a very short, eminently readable account of Zen practice in the Soto Zen tradition, there is none better than *An Introduction to the Tradition of Serene Reflection Meditation* (Mount Shasta, CA: Shasta Abbey Press, 1997). Excellent introductions to Zen Buddhism include *Zen Keys: A Guide to Zen Practice* by Thich Nhat Hanh (Berkeley, CA: Parallax Press, 1995), and Shunryo Suzuki's *Zen Mind, Beginners' Mind* (New York: Weatherhill, 1970).

There has long been a place for Zen Buddhism in American hearts, and a highly acclaimed investigation of Zen teaching in America is to be found in Helen Tworkov, *Zen in America. Five teachers and the Search for an American Buddhism* (New York, Tokyo, London: Kodansha International, 1994). A former journalist, *Roshi* Philip Kapleau is also eminently readable and his epic work *The Three Pillars of Zen*, which has been translated into ten languages, was republished in English recently (New York: Doubleday, 2000). Among other works by Kapleau are to be found *Zen* (London: Rider, 1980) and *Zen: Merging of East and West* (New York: Anchor Doubleday, 1989). *Zen Teaching, Zen Practice* (New York: Weatherhill, 2000), edited by Kenneth Kraft, is a tribute to *The Three Pillars of Zen* with contributions from eleven different writers.

There are also books dedicated to the poignant sayings of Zen masters. These collections include *Two Zen Classics: Mumonkan and Hekiganroku*, translated by Katsuki Sekida (New York: Weatherhill, 1996. First published 1977), *Moon in a Dewdrop: Writings of Zen Master Dogen* edited by Kasuaki Tanahashi (San Francisco: North Point Press, 1985), and *Zen Flesh, Zen Bones: A Collection of Zen and Pre-Zen Writings* by Paul Reps (Garden City, New York: Anchor Press, 1961). Another such book is *Zen's Chinese Heritage: The Masters and their Teachings* by Andy Ferguson (Boston; Wisdom, 2000), as is *The Old Zen Master: inspirations for awakening* by Trevor Leggett (Totnes: Buddhist Publishing Group, 2000). Earlier, we heeded Philip Kapleau's warning that reading about Zen is like studying the menu, whilst Zen practice is the eating of the meal. Trevor Leggett uses a comparable simile, though he prefers to equate books like *The Old Master* with pepper and salt. His point is that no amount of reading can replace solid practice!

If we didn't know better, when recommending further reading, it would not seem unreasonable to suggest that the reader begins with books that record the history of Zen, but strictly speaking there can be no "History of Zen". Zen masters had no interest in history, being more concerned with the needs of others than the deeds of themselves. Nor were Zen masters ever idolized as in other religions; there is no such thing as *roshi* worship in Zen. Consequently, Buddhist teachings were never considered to be literal truth, but as collections of useful ideas that may well point the way to truth, but actually have no historical warrant. This is how we should regard the case of Nansen Osho supposedly cutting the cat in half.

Nevertheless, it is Heinrich Dumoulin's two-volume work that is generally considered to be the definitive word on the history of Zen Buddhism: see H. Dumoulin *Zen Buddhism. A History. Volume 1, India and China* (London, New York: Macmillan, 1988), and *Zen Buddhism. A History. Volume 2, Japan* (London and New York: Macmillan, 1990). An earlier abridged version of these volumes is to be found in *A History of Zen Buddhism* (London: Faber and Faber, 1963) by the same author. The history of Rinzai Zen Buddhism is detailed in Martin Colcutt's *Five Mountains: the Rinzai Zen Monastic Institution in Medieval Japan* (Cambridge, MA: Harvard University Press, 1981). A full analysis of the place of the *koan* is given in *The Zen Koan: Its history and Use in Rinzai Zen* by Miura Isshu and Ruth Fuller Sasaki (New York: Harcourt, Brace and World, 1965). The Five Houses of Zen, which arose in China during the Golden Age of Zen are the subject of Thomas Cleary's work, unsurprisingly entitled *The Five Houses of Zen* (Boston, MA: Shambhala, 1997).

Zen Enlightenment: Origins and Meanings by Heinrich Dumoulin (New York: Weatherhill, 1979) is a classic study of the understanding of enlightenment in the history of Zen Buddhism, as is D. T. Suzuki's *The Zen Doctrine of No Mind* (London: Rider. First published 1949). The title of Dumoulin's *Zen Buddhism in the Twentieth Century* (New York: Weatherhill, 1992) speaks for itself, as does the erudition of the author. The Chinese relationship between

Taoism and Zen Buddhism is examined in Jeaneane Fowler's, *Pathways to Immortality: An Introduction to the Philosophy and Religion of Taoism* (Brighton and Portland: Sussex Academic Press, 2005).

For those interested in the psychology of Zen Buddhism, the reader is recommended Hubert Benoit's *The Supreme Doctrine*. Originally published in French in two volumes in 1951 and 1952, the work has recently been translated from the French by Graham Rooth in what is a superb new translation. See H. Benoit, *The Light of Zen in the West*, incorporating *The Supreme Doctrine* and *The Realization of the Self* (Brighton and Portland: Sussex Academic Press, 2004). An interesting recent paper on Zen and psychoanalysis is John Koller's "Buddhist and Psychoanalytic Insights into the Self and Self-awareness" in F. Hoffman and G. Mishra (eds) *Breaking Barriers: Essays in Asian and Comparative Philosophy* (Freemont CA: Asian Humanities Press, 2003). The reader who wishes to see Zen Buddhism within the broader context of the Asian mind is referred to *Asian Philosophies* by the same author (New Jersey: Prentice-Hall, fourth edn 2002. First published under the title *Oriental Philosophies* by Charles Scribner, 1970). On a lighter note, readers with a sense of humour will find *The Compass of Zen* by Zen Master Seung Sahn (New York, London: Shambhala, 1997) an hilarious presentation of the essential teachings of Zen.

Index

Amida/Amidhism, 95, 132
Ananda, 43, 81, 130
anapanasati, 111
anatta (Pali) (Skt. *anatman*), 53, 54, 57, 112
anicca (Pali) (Skt. *anitya*), 57, 112
arahant (Pali) (Skt. *arhat*), 44, 55, **64, 65,** 79
archery, 97, 102
Aryadeva, 81
Atisa, 135
Avalokitesvara (Chin. Kuan-yin; Jap. Kwannon/Kanzeon; Tibetan Chenre-zig), 119
Avatamsaka Sutras, 95

Bankai, 103
Basho, 98
Benoit, Hubert, 6
Bhavana, 110
Bhavacakra (wheel of becoming), 52–53
Blue Cliff Record (Jap. *Hekiganroku*), 96, 132
Bodhicitta, 101
Bodhidharma, 70, **79–83,** 86, 127
bodhisattva, 34, 35, 39, 70, 77, 89, 101
Book of Serenity, 96
Brahma-vihara, 66
Buddha, 6, 7, 26, 27, **31–43, 45–67**
Buddhacarita, 32–43
Buddha-nature/Buddhahood, 13, 21, 70, 80, 85, 101, 113, 114, 119, 122, 123, 127, 128, 130, 134, 136, 141, 145

Ch'an, **78–96,** 100, 109, 126
China, 7, 8, 13, 72, 76–**96,** 97, 113, 142

Chuan-Tzu, 126
Chu-chih, 90
citta, 111
Confucious/Confucianism, 76, 77, 78, 88, 91, 95, 97, 119

Three defilements/grenades, 46, 60, 65, 109, 116, 118, 138
delusion/deluded mind, **2–9,** 13, 47, 60, 109, 115, 116, 127
dhamma (Pali) (Skt. *dharma*), 29, 37, 39, 41, 42, 44, **45–67,** 69, 81, 87, 89, 95, 99, 102, 104, 110, 111, 116, 135, 136
Dhammapada, 58, 59, 61, 63
Dharma (mind) seal *(inka),* 81, 82, **86,** 100, 102, 136
dhyana, 48, **65,** 70, 77, 109, 110
Diamond Sutra, 70, 84, 90
Dogen Kigen (1200–1253), 8, **101–102,** 113, 116, 127, 130, 145
dokusan, 140
dualism/duality, 2, 19, 20, 23, 40, 73, 83, 90, 114, 117, 128, 136
dukkha (Pali) (Skt. *duhkha*), 45, **46–60**
Dosho, 98
Dumoulin, Heinrich, 79, 80, 97, 109

ego, 8, 23, 39, 65, **109,** 111, 112, 113, 114, 119, 126, 138, 144, 145
Eiheiji, 119
Eisei, Myoan, **99–100,** 101
Emperor Hsaio-ming, 82
Emperor Wu, 81
Emperor Wu-tsung, 89, 95
empty/emptiness, 21, 22, 69, 72, 73, 87, 93, 127, 130, 138

Enlightenment, 5, 6, 31, **32–43**, 44, 45, 56, 60, 84, 86, 87, 91, 95, 98, 99, 101, 102, 103, 104, 113, 114, 125, 134, 140
gradual enlightenment, 84
sudden enlightenment, 84, 142
Enni Ben'en, 100

House of Fa-yen, 94
fencing, 97
Fire Sermon, 135
five aggregates – see *skandhas*
The Five Houses of Zen, 92–95
Five Ranks, 88, 127
Four Noble Truths, 7, 45, **46–60**, 137
Fukanzazengi, 102

Goi, 127
goroku, 87
guru, 138, 139

Haikuin Ekaku, **103–104**, 122, 127
Haiku poetry, **97–98**, 102
Han dynasty, 77, 78, 79
Heart Sutra, 70
Heian period, 99
Hinayana, 77, 91
ho (Jap. *katsu*), 89
Hossin (Ultimate Reality), 127
Hosso, 99
Hotoke, 98
Hsuan tse, 85
Huai-jang, 88, 89
hua-hu, 87
Huang-Lao, 88
Huang-lung (Jap. Oryo), 100
Huang-po Hsi-yuan (Obaku Kiun) 91
Hua-yen (Jap. Kegon), 95
Hui-k'o, 82–84
Hui-neng, **84–86**, 89, 91, 92, 93, 142
Hung-jen, 84

ignorance, 37, 40, 47, 50, 52, 53, 57, 70, 76
Ikkyu Sojun, 102
Instruction for the Tenzo (Head Cook), 102
intuition/ intuitive knowledge, 11, 30, 83, 90, 109, 114, 128, 132, 141

Japan, 8, **97–105**, 137, 138, 140, 141
jakugo, 131,
Joshu, 127–130
Ju-ching, 102
judo, 97
jukai, 123

Kalyanamitta, 135
Kamakura period, 99, 100
kami cults, 98
kamma (Pali) (Skt. *karma*), 31, 39, 40, 42, 50, 51, 55, 58, **59**, 62, 77
karate, 97
karuna (compassion), 23, **66–67**, 119
kaya, 111
Kegon, 99
Keizan, 117
Kei-shan Ling Yu (Isan Reiyu), 91
Reverend Master Jiyu-Kennett, 117, **137–140**
Kenninji, 101, 102
kensho, 8, **114–15**, 134
ketchimyaku, 123
khandas (Pali) (Skt. *skandhas*)/ five aggregates, 50–51
Kikan, 127
kinhin, 113, 122
koan, 96, 100, 104, 109, 122, **125– 33**, 138, 140
Korea, 71, 72, 84, 98, 138
Koshohorinji, 102
House of Kuei-yang, 93
ku-ku-ku, 70
Kumarajiva, 78
kung fu, 97
Kwannon (Chin. Kwanyin), 119
Kyojukaimon, 116, 118
kyosaku, 140

lama, 138
lamp anthologies, 89, 91
Lankavatara sutra, 69, 71, 83, 84
Lao-tzu, 87
Liang dynasty, 82
liberation, 38
Lin-chi (Rinzai), 88, 92, 100
Lotus Sutra, 69, 70, 77, 99
loving kindness, 23

Madhyamaka, 70, 72, 73
mahakaruna, 69
Mahakasyapa, 81, 127, 136
Mahaparinibbana sutta, 130.
Mahaprajnaparamita sutta, 70
Mahasanghika, 68
Mahayana, 7, **68–75**, 76, 77, 92
mandalas, 103, 122
mantra, 122
Mappo, 99, 102
master–disciple relationship, 8, 84, 104, 134–42

Ma-tsu, 8, 89, 91, 92
meditation, 2, 8, 16, 17, 20, 24, 60, 70, 71,
    72, 77, 79, 81, 82, 83, 89, 91, 97, 98,
    99, 102, 103, 104, **109–25, 143–48**
Meiji period, 88, 104
metaphysics, 26, 68, 71, 76, 90, 101, 129
metta, 66–67
monks/monasteries, 23, 26, 44, 46, 62, 63,
    70, 71, 72, 76, 80, 84, 89, 91, 96, 98,
    99, 100, 101, 104, 110, 113, **117–24**,
    136, 137, 141, 146
mondo, 83, 132
monism, 29

Reverend Master Daishin Morgan, 5, 117,
    137, 144
mu/wu, 104, 127, **128–30**
mudita, 66–67
Mumon Ekai, 128
Mumonkan (The Gateless Gate), 90, 96,
    127, **128–30**, 132, 136
Myozen, 101
Mysticism, 26

Nagarjuna, 73, 81
Nansen Osho, 89
nembutsu, 96, 132
nibbana (Pali) (Skt. *nirvana*), 40, 41, 44,
    46, 55, 56, 59, **60**, **65**, 69, 110, 123
Nichiren, 99
Noble Eightfold Path, 7, **49–67**
non-being, 128, 129
Northern/Southern Schools, 84, 85

Order of Buddhist Contemplatives
    (O.B.C.), 137
Ox-herding Pictures, 7, **13–24**, 144

Pai-chang, 76, 91
Pali/Pali Canon, 30, 31, 48, 71
Pancha Sila, **59–63**
panna (Pali) (Skt. *prajna*)/wisdom, 56, **57**,
    63–64, **67**, 69, 70, 109, 110
parinibbana (Pali) (Skt. *parinirvana*), 31,
    41
paramitas, 69, 79
Patanjali, 74
paticcasamuppada, 53–55
patriarchs, 26, 71, 72, 80, 81, 82, 83, 84, 85,
    122, 127
philosophy, 26, 68, 73, 83, 95, 99
Prajnaparamita (Pefection of Wisdom), 7,
    68, 69, 70, 72, 73
Precepts, 16, 59, 62, 63, 116

Pure Land, 95, 99, 101, 132

realization, 30, 43, 45, 49
Record of the Transmission of the Lamp,
    79, 86
Three Refuges/Jewels, 45, 116
retreat, 4
Rinzai Zen, 88, 89, 90, **93**, 95, 96, **97**, 99,
    100, 101, 102, 104, 122, 123, 127, 133,
    140, 141
Rinzairoku, 90
roshi, 140

Sakyamuni, 6, 26, 80, 81
salvation, 6
samadhi, **57**, **63–67**, 110, **115**
samatha, 110, 111
samsara, 7, 31, 39, 42, 45, 46, 47, 55, 57,
    87, 115, 122
Samurai, 97, 102, 141
Samyutta Nikaya, 135
sangha, 44, 68, 95, 116, 137
Ruth Fuller Sasaki, 126
Satipatthana sutta, 111
satori, 8, 83, 104, 109, **113–15**, 123, 126,
    129, 131, 145,
Serene Reflection Meditation, **116**, 120,
    146
sesshin, , 113, 118
Shasta Abbey, 137
Shaku Soen, 104
Shen-hui, 84, 85
Shen-hsiu, 84
Shih-t'ou, 89, 92
shikantaza, 96, 122.
Shingon, 99, 100, 101, 103
Shinto, 104
Shobogenzo, 102, 130
Shofokugi, 100
Shotoku Taishi, 98
sila, 63–64
Five *skandhas/aggregates*, 49–58
Son, 71, 72
Soto Zen, 8, 26, 88, **94**, 95, 96, 101, 102,
    104, 113, **116–24**, 137
stick-and-shout, 89, 101, 102
suffering, 45, **46–60**
Sumitra, 137
Sung dynasty, 13, 80, 88, **95–96**, 104
Sung-Yun, 82
sunya, 70
sunyata, 7, 71, **72–73**, 78, 87, 130
sutta (Pali) (Skt. *sutra*) ,61
Sutta Pitaka , 137

Suzuki, D. T, 7, 25, 26, 70, 71, 73, 74, 105, 113, 117, 126, 132, 133, 137
svabhava, 72, 73

T'ai Chi Ch'uan, 87
T'ang dynasty, 80, 86, 88, 90, 92, 94, 95, 104
Tanha (craving), **54, 55, 57**, 58
Tantra, 138
Tao, 1, 79, 129
Tao-hsuan, 83
Tao-hsin, 84, 91
tao-te, 79
Taoism, 73, 77, 78, 79, 83, 86, 87, 88, 95, 96, 97, 123, 126
Tathagata, 6, 41, 43, 83
Ta-wei, 93
Tea ceremony, 97, 102, 103
Tendai (Chin. T''ien-tai), 76, 95, 99, 100, 101
Tendo Nyojo, 110
Tenzo (Head Cook), 102
Te-shan (Tokusan), 90
Throssel Hole Soto Zen Priory, 5, 114, **117–24**, 137
Tien-t'ung-szu monastery, 102
Tipitaka (Pali) (Skt. *Tripitaka*), 61
Tung-shan, 88
Ts'oa-tung (Soto Zen), 88

Ultimate Reality/Truth, 27, 30, 31, 38, 40, 47, 48, **56**, 60, 69, 73, 111, 114, 123, 127
unsui, 119
Upanisads, **29–30**, 46, 47, 74, 131

upaya , 90, 93
upekkha, 66–67

vedana, 111
Vimalikirti Sutra, 89, 98
Vinaya Pitaka, 76, 110
Vipassana, 110, 111

Wesak, 137
Western Ch'an, 122, 126, 128, 141
wisdom, 23, 47, 51, 58, 64, 87, 90
Wu-men Hui-k'ai, 130, 136
wu-wei, 79, 97, 123, 129

yana, 129
yang, 1
Yang-shan, 93
yin, 1
yoga, 7, 38, 60, **73–75**, 110
Yogacara, 65, 70
House of Yun-men, 94

zazen, 8, 100, 102, 109, **113–14**, 116, 117, 120, 122, 128, 140
zafu, 120
zendo, 119, 120, 121, 141, 146
Zen Garden, 124

"Does a dog have Buddha nature?"

The author pictured with his confidant,
Copperfield
(Kennel name "Corriebran Chayton")

Personal Notes

Personal Notes

Personal Notes

Personal Notes

Personal Notes

Personal Notes

Personal Notes

Personal Notes